THE
SEVEN PRINCIPLES FOR
PROFESSIONAL EXCELLENCE

IBRAHIM S. EMRAN

FIRST EDITION

Title: The Seven Principles for Professional Excellence

Author: Ibrahim Emran
Reviewer: Abdallah Emran
Proofreader: Sarah Emran

For feedback or permission requests related to this book, please contact the author through the following channels:

Email: info@the7principles.net
Website: www.the7principles.net

ISBN: 979-8-9922-1380-5

To my late parents, who instilled in me the core values that have shaped my life. To my lovely wife and beloved children, whose endless encouragement and inspiration have been my greatest strength. To my sisters, whose joy at this book's realization has filled me with great pride. And to all the individuals who have enriched my personal and professional journey—thank you.

Table of Contents

Introduction

Welcome to "The Seven Principles for Professional Excellence," a transformative reading journey that promises to redefine your approach to professional success and personal growth. This book is a treasure trove of insights, derived from over three decades of experience across a diverse range of sectors—including private and public entities, as well as for-profit and non-profit organizations, including a Fortune 100 company. It is crafted to guide readers through each phase of their career development.

In today's fast-paced and ever-evolving job market, mastering soft skills is crucial for professional success. This book serves as an indispensable crash course in these essential skills, universally applicable and without boundaries. Catering to a broad spectrum of readers—from high school students embarking on their initial professional experiences to college students exploring the complexities of professional behavior, from recent graduates eager to make a significant impact to seasoned executives looking to refine their expertise, and entrepreneurs striving to expand their ventures—this guide offers crucial support for excelling in the dynamic professional world. Each reader will interpret and utilize these skills uniquely based on their individual experiences, goals, and professional perspectives. Additionally, the book provides key insights for standing out in job interviews, ensuring readers are well-prepared to present their best selves to potential employers.

This book is a mind-opener, revealing the changes you can make and the actions you can take to significantly impact your life. Mastering the competencies and skills required for a professional lifestyle is essential, and how well you integrate and apply these skills will determine their effect on your personal and professional development.

Throughout my career, I have had the opportunity to report to more than fifteen direct managers—ranging from senior-level professionals to executives—each with a distinct management style. The leaders I admired most were those who truly contributed to my professional development. Their impactful leadership provided valuable strategies and served as key examples of excellence. These experiences have profoundly shaped the insights and methodologies presented in this book, reflecting a wide range of leadership dynamics that resonate across diverse corporate cultures.

In this book, we delve into seven core competencies, each crucial for professional success and personal growth:

1. **Time Management: Stay Focused** — Learn how to effectively manage your time, prioritize tasks, and set clear professional and personal goals. By establishing a focused direction, you will boost productivity and stay aligned with your objectives, ensuring steady progress toward success.

2. **Interpersonal Communication** — Master the art of communication, including perception, self-esteem, active listening, and understanding non-verbal cues, to build stronger, more constructive relationships, both professionally and personally.

3. **Organizational Culture: Living the Values** — Discover the importance of aligning with your organization's culture, embodying its values, and contributing to a positive and ethical workplace.

4. **Conducting Effective Meetings** — Learn how to organize and lead meetings that are efficient, inclusive, and designed to drive decisions and foster collaboration.

5. **Effective Negotiation** — Develop the skills for successful negotiation, focusing on win-win outcomes that respect and satisfy all parties involved.

6. **Problem-Solving and Decision-Making** — Equip yourself with strategies to tackle complex challenges and make informed decisions with confidence and clarity.

7. **Finance for Non-Finance Professionals** — Gain essential financial literacy by mastering the fundamentals of finance, including understanding, creating, and managing budgets, as well as performing accurate forecasting.

While these competencies form the foundation of professional excellence, they are only the beginning. Mastering these skills is the first step toward advancing in your career and evolving into an outstanding leader. In the workplace, promotions and advancements often come with higher expectations, and while some may rise through seniority alone, without these fundamental soft skills, they risk being unprepared and facing setbacks.

The inspiration for writing this book came from my experience leading numerous technical and soft skills workshops. Time and again, I observed significant gaps in essential professional skills that hindered performance and peer relationships. Unfortunately, traditional education and training programs often fail to address these gaps, leading to missed opportunities and professional challenges. This book is designed to bridge those gaps, equipping readers with the tools they need not just to succeed, but to excel.

The feedback received from workshop participants has significantly boosted my motivation. Many shared the view that such workshops should be accessible to all employees within their organizations to cultivate a uniform understanding of professionalism. A frequent reflection among attendees was the regret of not having these skills introduced earlier in their educational or professional journey. This book aims to address that gap by reaching a wider audience and providing essential lessons at an earlier stage. Additionally, it serves as an invaluable tool for college practicum courses, equipping students with the knowledge and skills needed to meet the expectations of professional life.

A personal story that underscores the need for professionalism involves my daughter, who faced a dilemma when selecting her university courses. She hesitated to enroll in a class taught by a professor known for his inconsistency—mood swings that could affect the learning environment. This experience serves as a reminder of the importance of fairness and professionalism, qualities that can define or derail one's experience in education or the workplace.

This book is designed to be accessible, engaging, and practical. The narrative is crafted to draw readers in with relatable examples, practical advice, and actionable insights. Whether you read it in a week or take your time over a month, each chapter offers lessons that can be immediately applied. My goal is not just to inform, but to transform—encouraging readers to internalize and master each skill until it becomes a natural part of their professional and personal lives.

To effectively master these skills, honest self-reflection is essential. It is crucial to evaluate whether your current environment—be it the people surrounding you, your workplace, or even your living situation—fosters the changes you aspire to implement. Identifying and overcoming any barriers is key to fully utilizing these competencies and achieving both personal and professional growth.

My aim is not just to share knowledge but to inspire an ongoing journey of development. This book is structured to be a lifelong resource—each chapter can stand alone, offering flexibility to read based on your immediate needs. Whether you are working through the chapters sequentially or turning to a section that addresses a current challenge, this guide is a valuable companion throughout your career.

As we journey through "The Seven Principles for Professional Excellence," you will discover that true success goes beyond individual accomplishments. It involves contributing to a larger vision, leading with integrity, and inspiring excellence in those around you. By mastering these essential competencies, you will elevate your career and make a lasting impact on your team, your organization, and your community. These skills extend beyond the workplace, enriching personal interactions and transforming every facet of your life.

I invite you to join me on this transformative journey. Together, we will explore these principles and apply them to carve a path toward genuine, lasting professional excellence. Let this book be your guide as you navigate the complexities of today's workplace and life, continually learning, growing, and achieving with each chapter and every experience.

Chapter One

Time Management: Stay Focused

A t the beginning of our exploration of Time Management: Stay Focused, it is vital to acknowledge that everyone operates within the same 24-hour day. While some individuals manage to achieve remarkable achievements within this time, others may find themselves making less significant progress. The encouraging news is that mastering the balance of life and focusing on important goals and activities is indeed achievable. Keeping your personal and professional goals aligned makes it possible to harness your time effectively, regardless of how late in life you start this practice.

This chapter underscores the essence of staying focused and maintaining your directional compass aligned, which are pivotal to successful time management.

Time management goes beyond simple discipline; it is the art of crafting processes and tools that enhance efficiency and effectiveness in all aspects of life, both personal and professional. Unlike innate talent, time management is a skill cultivated through consistent effort and ongoing practice. For many, this endeavor is a lifelong challenge, emphasizing the importance of utilizing every moment productively and in harmony with one's overarching goals.

Consider the process of mastering time management as similar to learning a martial art: it requires refining your techniques over time, with consistent practice and dedication to repeating foundational concepts until they embed deeply into your routine. Effective time management is vital across all walks of life. Whether you are a student juggling academic responsibilities and social engagements, a professional managing multiple projects, or a business owner coordinating daily operations and strategic planning, mastering this skill is crucial. It plays a pivotal role in maintaining a balanced lifestyle and achieving success in every facet of one's endeavors.

The Importance of Time

Time is our most valuable resource—limited, irreplaceable, and always moving forward. Unlike money or material possessions, it cannot be earned, bought, or recovered once lost.

To truly grasp the value of time, consider how even a brief moment can change everything:

- A student who must repeat an entire year due to a single failed exam.

- A mother whose baby arrives a month earlier than expected.

- An athlete who finishes just milliseconds short of winning gold.

Each situation reveals the same truth: every second matters.

One of the most powerful real-life illustrations is the story of US Airways Flight 1549. In January 2009, Captain Chesley "Sully" Sullenberger had just 35 seconds to make a life-or-death decision after both engines failed. His successful emergency landing on the Hudson River saved all 155 passengers on board. It was a testament to how crucial clear thinking and time management can be—when every second counts.

Time, when managed well, becomes a powerful tool for success. When overlooked, it quietly slips away—taking opportunities with it.

Obstacles to Effective Time Management

Many people struggle with time management not due to a lack of effort, but because they lack clarity about what truly matters. Without clear priorities, it's easy to fall into a reactive pattern—constantly responding to emails, attending meetings, and handling requests—without making meaningful progress on core objectives.

A common obstacle is the inability to say "no." Samar, a talented software engineer, was widely respected for her willingness to support others. Her calendar quickly filled with unscheduled support sessions, last-minute tasks, and team issues—none of which aligned with her primary responsibilities. Although she felt busy and engaged, her own project deadlines began to slip, and her stress levels rose. Over time, Samar realized that her eagerness to help was undermining her effectiveness. By setting clear boundaries and learning to prioritize, she regained control of her time and improved her performance without sacrificing her well-being.

Additional challenges include perfectionism—spending too much time fine-tuning minor details—and the misconception that multitasking leads to greater efficiency. In reality, switching between tasks disrupts focus, increases the chance of errors, and contributes to mental fatigue. True productivity stems from giving full attention to one priority at a time.

Lastly, while urgency can sometimes fuel motivation, consistently working under pressure takes a toll. It diminishes mental clarity, impairs decision-making, and affects overall well-being. Long-term success is not about working faster, but about working smarter—with thoughtful planning, balance, and the discipline to pause and refocus when needed.

Time Planning

Time management is often likened to the cornerstone of personal and professional success. It is a skill that, when mastered, allows individuals to navigate the complexities of modern life with confidence and clarity.

For instance, consider the story of a successful entrepreneur, John. John started his first business in his early twenties, full of energy and ambition, but he quickly found himself overwhelmed by the demands on his time. Every day was a struggle to keep up with meetings, manage employees, handle client requests, and still find time to innovate and grow his business. John understood that without mastering time management, he risked burning out before his business could achieve success.

John decided to take a step back and reassess how he was spending his time. He began by identifying the tasks most critical to his business's success and made a conscious effort to delegate or eliminate less-essential activities. By setting clear, measurable goals and creating a daily schedule aligned with those objectives, John brought greater structure and focus to his work. He also set aside time for regular reflection and adjustments, which enabled continuous improvement. Within a year, his business saw remarkable growth, and he achieved a more balanced and fulfilling work-life routine. John's journey stands as a compelling example of the transformative power of effective time management.

Another example comes from the life of Maria, a university student juggling her studies, part-time job, and social life. Initially, Maria struggled with procrastination, often leaving her assignments until the last minute. This led to stress and below-average grades. Realizing she needed to change, Maria began to implement time management strategies such as breaking her study sessions into focused intervals using the Pomodoro Technique—a method where you work for 25 minutes followed by a 5-minute break. She also set clear deadlines for herself and prioritized her tasks based on importance and urgency. As a result, Maria's grades improved, and she found more time to enjoy her hobbies and friendships.

Planning is not just about creating a to-do list; it is about creating a roadmap that guides your actions and decisions. Successful planning starts with setting clear, long-term goals. For example, if your goal is to advance in your career, your plan might include gaining new skills, seeking out mentorship, and taking on challenging projects. Once these long-term goals are established, they need to be broken down into smaller, actionable steps.

Another crucial aspect of planning is tracking your tasks once you have clearly defined the main goal you are trying to achieve. Utilizing the right tools and systems to stay organized can greatly enhance your time management. Whether it is a digital calendar, project management software, or a simple notebook, these tools can significantly impact your efficiency.

Another key aspect of planning is flexibility. While it is important to have a plan, it is equally important to be able to adapt when things do not go as expected. Sarah, the marketing executive, learned this lesson when one of her major campaigns was suddenly put on hold due to unforeseen circumstances. Rather than seeing this as a setback, Sarah used the opportunity to focus on other projects that had been on the back burner.

Sarah's ability to pivot and adapt her plans allowed her to continue making progress, even when her original plan had to be adjusted. This example illustrates the importance of being both strategic and flexible in your planning, ensuring that you are always moving forward, even in the face of challenges.

Time Control

Time control is a concept that emphasizes an important truth: while we can manage many aspects of our lives, there are external factors beyond our control. These may include the actions of others, unexpected events, natural disasters, or economic downturns. Recognizing this distinction is essential for effective time management, as it helps us focus our energy on what we can influence, rather than being overwhelmed by what we cannot.

For example, consider a scenario where someone's job starts at eight in the morning—a start time they cannot change. This person might often complain about waking up early and not getting enough sleep. However, focusing on the uncontrollable start time of their job is unproductive. Instead, what they can control is the time they go to bed. By adjusting their bedtime, they can ensure they get enough sleep, thus taking control of the situation. This adjustment improves their well-being and enhances their time management by focusing on what they can influence rather than what is out of their control.

Although we cannot control everything, we can control how we respond to these external factors. A key aspect of time control is recognizing the difference between actions and consequences. While we can choose our actions, the consequences of those actions are often governed by external forces. For example, you might choose to spend time preparing for a presentation, but the outcome, such as the audience's reception, might not be entirely within your control.

When faced with challenges beyond our control, it is crucial to adopt a strategic approach that involves three key actions: acceptance, adaptation, and redirection. Acceptance requires recognizing the reality of the situation and understanding that certain factors are beyond our influence. Adaptation involves modifying our plans or strategies to better align with the new circumstances. Lastly, redirection entails shifting our focus away from the uncontrollable elements and channeling our efforts towards areas where we can make a difference. This systematic approach allows us to effectively manage obstacles and maintain progress.

A compelling analogy to understand these responses is depicted in the story of the coffee bean, popularized by Jon Gordon and Damon West in their book "The Coffee Bean." They delineate three distinct reactions to adversity, symbolized by a carrot, an egg, and a coffee bean in boiling water. The carrot softens and becomes weak, reflecting those who let challenges diminish their spirit. The egg hardens, symbolizing individuals who grow bitter and inflexible when faced with hardships. In contrast, the coffee bean transforms its environment, illustrating the profound impact of a proactive mindset that enables one to influence their surroundings rather than being subdued by them.

One of the most recent and profound examples of external challenges is the COVID-19 pandemic, which disrupted lives and economies worldwide. This global crisis was a reminder of the importance of focusing on what we can control—our health, our actions, and our response to the situation—rather than being paralyzed by what we cannot control.

Time Matrix

The Time Matrix, also known as the Eisenhower Matrix (Figure 1), is a powerful tool for managing time and prioritizing tasks. It categorizes tasks based on two dimensions: urgency and importance. By organizing tasks in this way, individuals can focus on what truly matters rather than being consumed by less important activities.

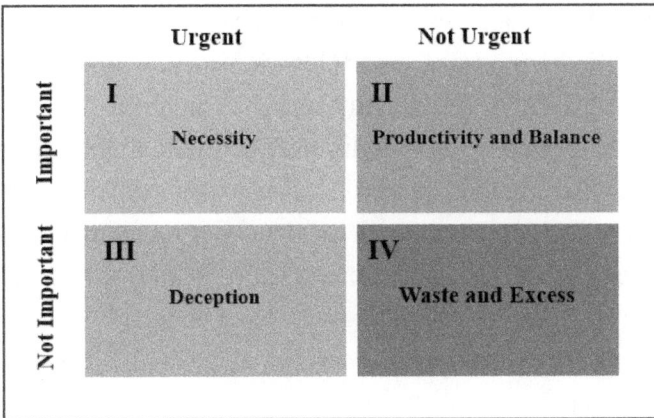

	Urgent	**Not Urgent**
Important	**I** Necessity	**II** Productivity and Balance
Not Important	**III** Deception	**IV** Waste and Excess

Figure 1. Eisenhower Matrix

The matrix is divided into four quadrants:

Quadrant I: Necessity (Important and Urgent) – This quadrant includes crises, pressing problems, and deadline-driven projects. Tasks in this category require immediate attention and cannot be postponed.

Quadrant II: Productivity and Balance (Important but Not Urgent) – Tasks in this quadrant are essential for long-term success. They include planning, prevention, relationship building, and personal development. Although not urgent, these tasks are crucial for achieving meaningful goals.

Quadrant III: Deception (Not Important but Urgent) – This quadrant includes activities that appear urgent but are not truly important. These tasks often feel pressing because they are important to others, not necessarily to you. Examples include interruptions, some meetings, and minor issues that can be delegated or ignored.

15

Quadrant IV: Waste and Excess (Not Important and Not Urgent) –This quadrant includes activities that are largely unproductive and serve as timewasters, such as excessive TV watching, prolonged social media use, or other distractions that do not support your goals or priorities. For example, watching TV can be categorized as a Quadrant I or II activity when it is a way to unwind after a long day, take a break, or reward yourself. However, in this context, we are referring to excessive TV watching that detracts from productivity and does not align with your objectives.

The challenge of time management often arises from the tendency of many individuals to spend an excessive amount of time on tasks that may feel urgent but do not align with their long-term goals (often referred to as Quadrant III activities). These tasks provide a sense of busyness and self-importance but do not contribute to substantial growth or productivity. In contrast, high achievers prioritize Quadrant II activities, dedicating time to essential tasks that foster growth and balance, recognizing their importance, and tackling them promptly and without complaint.

Sometimes, the urgency of tasks is compounded by directives from superiors, who may themselves be acting under orders. For example, a manager might assign an urgent task because their own superior has deemed it urgent, yet never follow up on it. This frequent occurrence in many organizations highlights a fundamental problem with prioritizing and following through on tasks, potentially leading to operational bottlenecks and disruptions in future workflows.

This approach was vividly illustrated during a consultancy I conducted for an organization where we asked each employee and department to list their daily and weekly tasks along with the time dedicated to each. One encounter stands out: I reminded a manager to complete his forms, a task that should not have taken more than 15 to 30 minutes. However, he spent nearly an hour discussing his past achievements and justifying his busy schedule, which he claimed prevented him from completing the forms. This experience highlighted how mismanagement of time and unclear priorities can lead to inefficiency, even among those who perceive themselves as highly busy and important.

The story of President Dwight D. Eisenhower, from whom the matrix gets its name, is a prime example of effective time management. As the 34th President of the United States, Eisenhower had to prioritize and manage a multitude of tasks, from national security to economic policies. By using this matrix, he was able to focus on what was truly important, avoiding the distractions that could have derailed his administration.

The key point is to prioritize tasks based on their importance. To determine whether a task is critical, assess the consequences of its non-completion. If failing to complete the task results in significant negative outcomes, it is essential. Conversely, if there are minimal consequences, the task may not be as crucial. This prioritization ensures focus on tasks that have the most impact on overall success.

Starting Point

Effective time management begins with a solid foundation of planning. However, before delving into the details of planning, it is essential to engage in some honest self-reflection by asking a few critical questions: Have you truly reflected on the importance of time management? Are you prepared to embrace the changes necessary to enhance your productivity?

Acknowledging the importance of time management is the initial step. Without this recognition, any attempts at planning are likely to be ineffective. Equally crucial is the willingness to change. This readiness involves more than just adopting new methods or tools; it requires a commitment to honestly assess your current habits and circumstances. If you fail to admit that your approach to time management might be flawed, there is little incentive to seek improvement. Embracing change means being open to evaluating and adjusting your routines and strategies to achieve better time management outcomes.

Setting the Compass

Setting the compass refers to the process of defining your direction and goals. This is often referred to as the 'first creation,' which happens in your mind before any action is taken. It is about visualizing your end goals and setting a clear path to achieve them.

Setting goals is an essential part of this process. Whether it is a work project, personal development, education, better health, moving to a bigger house, planning for retirement, or even planning a vacation, having clear goals helps you stay focused and committed.

Setting the Plans

To ensure continued progress on the right path and achieve the goals you aspire to, it is essential to document these goals precisely. Written goals enhance commitment, keeping your ambitions alive in your mind, helping maintain motivation, facilitating periodic progress evaluations, preventing conflicts, and effectively organizing priorities. Additionally, job interviews often include questions about a candidate's personal strategic goals and aspirations, as employers, even for entry-level positions, are keen to understand the candidate's vision and long-term plans for the future.

Once you have a clear vision and well-defined long-term strategic goals, the next step is to translate them into actionable plans. Begin with a one-year plan, providing a high-level overview of your objectives for the year. Then, break this plan down further into smaller, manageable tasks, categorized by monthly, weekly, and daily tasks (Figure 2).

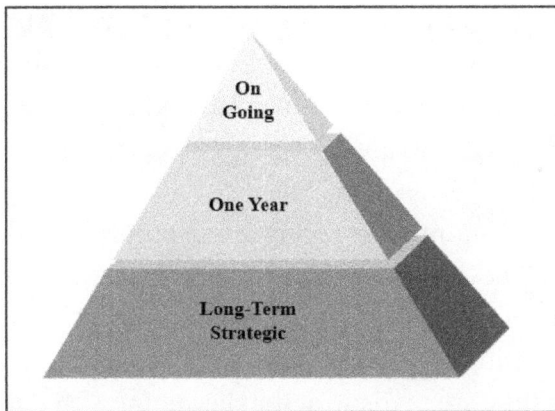

Figure 2. Planning Pyramid

On-going plans are crucial for maintaining momentum toward your long-term goals. These plans are typically reviewed on a monthly, weekly, and daily basis. At the beginning of each month or week, take time to review your tasks and make necessary adjustments. For daily tasks, it is helpful to review them the day before or early in the

19

morning to ensure that you are prepared. Always expect the unexpected. If you encounter tasks that cannot be completed as planned, be prepared to reschedule, delegate, or even cancel them if they are no longer necessary.

Each of these tasks should have a specific deadline and should be broken down into doable chunks. This approach ensures that you make steady progress toward your long-term goals without feeling overwhelmed. Regularly review and revise your plans as needed to stay on track and adjust to any changes or unforeseen challenges.

If someone aims to start their own business in five years with a long-term goal of saving $60,000, it is more effective to break this goal into smaller, trackable milestones rather than simply setting the target and waiting five years to assess progress. This approach provides a clear roadmap and ensures consistent progress toward the ultimate objective. They could aim to save $12,000 each year, which translates to saving an average of $1,000 per month.

By annually and monthly tracking their progress, individuals can gauge whether they are on course to achieve their long-term goals, making necessary adjustments to remain aligned. This systematic approach to setting, breaking down, and consistently monitoring goals ensures they are realistic and in harmony with the individual's overarching vision.

An effective way to structure your annual plans, both personally and professionally, is by using frameworks like Management by Objectives (MBO). The MBO approach offers a straightforward template for tracking your progress throughout the year (Figure 3).

While MBO is a widely recognized and successful strategy, it represents just one of the numerous tools available to ensure your goals are in alignment with your broader vision. Remember, these templates are flexible and can be customized to better suit your unique needs.

Management by Objectives (MBO) January 1 – December 31		
Goal # 1	**Due Date**	**Status**
1. SMART Objective		
2. SMART Objective		
3. SMART Objective		
4. SMART Objective		
Sample Goal: Enhance HR Skills As Measured By:	**Due Date**	**Status**
1. Conduct a detailed review of all current HR policies to ensure they align with the latest industry standards and legislative requirements.	March 31	
2. Attend a SHRM classroom workshop to enhance the professional HR knowledge.	June 30	
3. Read at least two recommended HR books to expand the understanding of HR compensation strategies.	September 30	
4. Deliver a one-hour presentation to the HR team to demonstrate the updated HR knowledge and effective communication skills.	December 31	

Figure 3. A Sample of Modified Management by Objectives (MBO)

SMART Goals

One of the most effective frameworks for setting and achieving goals is the SMART criteria. SMART stands for Specific, Measurable, Attainable, Relevant, and Time-bound. By following these guidelines, you can create clear and actionable objectives that are more likely to be achieved.

Specific: Goals should be well-defined and clear. Avoid vague language and ensure that everyone involved understands what needs to be accomplished.

Measurable: Establish concrete criteria for measuring progress. This could be in terms of quantity, quality, cost, or other relevant metrics, it is a matter of black and white, has it been accomplished or not.

Attainable: Goals should be realistic and achievable within the given timeframe and resources. They should push you to grow and improve but not be so unrealistic that they lead to frustration. At the same time, they should not be so easily attainable that they simply serve as items to check off your to-do list without providing meaningful progress.

Relevant: Goals should align with your overall objectives and be worthwhile. They should contribute meaningfully to your long-term plans.

Time-bound: Every goal should have a deadline. This helps create a sense of urgency and ensures that tasks are completed within a reasonable timeframe.

By applying the SMART framework, you can transform vague aspirations into clear, actionable goals. For example, consider the following SMART goals:

- Increase website traffic by 20% over the next three months by implementing a content marketing strategy, including weekly blog posts and social media promotion.

- Improve customer satisfaction scores by 15% within six months by enhancing customer support training and implementing new feedback system.

- Launch a new product by the end of Q2, achieving at least $100,000 in sales within the first three months post-launch.

These examples demonstrate how the SMART framework facilitates the establishment of goals that are clear, actionable, and aligned with broader objectives, thereby enhancing the likelihood of success. It is important to note that each goal must incorporate all five criteria of the SMART framework—Specific, Measurable, Attainable, Relevant, and Time-bound—to be considered complete and effective.

Planning Tips – Avoiding Time Conflicts

Planning is not just about setting goals; it is crucial for effectively managing your time to prevent conflicts. One highly beneficial practice is beginning the year by working with your annual personal calendar. This proactive approach allows you to visualize and organize your commitments and projects over the coming months. It is not merely scheduling but prioritizing what needs to be accomplished.

Additionally, encourage your team to submit their tentative annual plans early. This proactive approach will help ensure sufficient coverage during peak periods and facilitate better coordination of activities within the team. While emergencies can still arise, advance planning greatly reduces their impact.

During structured planning sessions, such as a 'Plan/Map Days,' it is important to anticipate potential interruptions and allocate time accordingly. Whether you use sticky notes, digital tools, or another method that suits your style, map out your tasks, objectives, and deadlines. This strategy does not just clarify priorities; it also aligns resources, prevents last-minute scrambles, and communicates expectations with all team members.

This methodical approach extends to personal life as well. For example, when planning a family vacation, consider everyone's schedules, available resources, and any possible scheduling conflicts. This mirrors a project management exercise, where thorough planning is essential for a smooth, successful outcome.

Leveraging Technology for Effective Planning

In the technology-driven era we live in, keeping your plans organized is more manageable than ever before. You have a wide range of software and applications at your disposal, so choose the one that best suits your personal preferences and needs. Whether it is a digital calendar, project management tool, or a simple note-taking app, the important thing is to select a platform that you are comfortable with and that integrates seamlessly into your daily routine.

Effective email management is a vital component of using technology to your advantage. Think of your email inbox as more than just a holding area—it is a workspace where efficiency can be maximized. Adopt the 4Ds approach for managing your emails: Do immediately respond to urgent and important messages, Delete unnecessary emails to keep your inbox clean, Defer responses to less urgent emails by scheduling a specific time for handling them, and Delegate tasks that can be handled by someone else.

Promptly responding to emails and promptly following up on missed calls reflects a high level of professionalism. Conversely, delays in responses or tasks, or ignoring communications, often indicate not just a busy schedule but an overwhelmed state and a struggle to keep up with your responsibilities. This proactive approach to email management streamlines your workflow and highlights your capability to maintain control and efficiency in your professional role.

Sharing calendars with your team is a highly effective feature that greatly enhances the efficiency and coordination of organizational operations. It ensures that all team members are aware of each other's schedules, which enhances coordination and respects individual time commitments. When scheduling any event, it is crucial to check these shared times to avoid conflicts and to honor the times that have already been set aside.

To achieve maximum efficiency, the technology you choose should be mobile-friendly, enabling access anytime and anywhere. Choose tools that seamlessly synchronize across multiple devices, allowing you to update and review your plans effortlessly, whether using a phone, tablet, or computer. Success depends on selecting the right tool and your dedication to using it consistently, as well as regularly monitoring your progress to stay aligned with your goals.

Summary

It is crucial to recognize that effective time management exceeds the simple scope of professional obligations; it fundamentally involves crafting a harmonious balance between achieving career objectives and enjoying personal fulfillment. This balanced approach empowers individuals to exercise greater control over their daily lives, leading to significant improvements in both productivity and personal satisfaction.

Effective time management enhances your efficiency in handling professional tasks and promotes engagement in activities that support personal growth and happiness.

Enhancing your time management skills enhances daily productivity, reduces stress, and improves overall well-being. This development is essential for maintaining an effective and balanced lifestyle. This approach is not about trying to pack more hours into the day; instead, it focuses on optimizing the hours you have.

By prioritizing essential tasks, you can minimize time spent on less critical activities, effectively freeing up more hours for fulfilling pursuits. Consider the impact of saving just one extra hour each day: over fifty years, this could add approximately two years to your productive life. Imagine the possibilities if you could apply various time management strategies to save and utilize even more time effectively.

Mastering time management involves working smarter to enhance productivity and personal satisfaction. The strategies outlined in this chapter are tailored to keep you focused and propel you toward your goals more efficiently. Implementing these techniques can lead to a more productive professional life and a more fulfilling personal life. Recognizing the value of each wisely spent minute is crucial for leading a balanced and enriched life.

Additionally, it is important to understand that you cannot truly excel professionally and personally until you commit to continual self-improvement. This means dedicating time to read, learn, and apply new skills—time that the techniques listed in this chapter can help you find. Every professional must actively work on themselves; otherwise, they risk becoming outdated. Fortunately, no excuses remain in today's world, with abundant resources at your fingertips, including online courses, paper and electronic books, and audiobooks. Committing to this additional effort is crucial for anyone striving to become a professional they can genuinely take pride in.

Chapter Two

Interpersonal Communication

I nterpersonal communication encompasses the exchange of information, ideas, feelings, and meanings among two or more individuals through both verbal and non-verbal methods. This form of communication is distinctive because it acknowledges others as unique individuals and typically involves mutual influence, often aimed at managing relationships. While this chapter does not specifically address public speaking, the interpersonal skills discussed are fundamental to various types of communication. Understanding your audience, communicating effectively, and projecting confidence are fundamental skills for successful public speaking.

Effective interpersonal communication improves relationships with family, friends, and colleagues and also enhances both physical and emotional health. Consider the strain of working daily with someone you find difficult; effective communication in such situations can significantly mitigate stress and increase productivity.

To illustrate, let us consider the story of two colleagues, Jennifer and Carl. Jennifer is new to the team and feels intimidated by the fast-paced environment. Carl, a seasoned team member, notices her hesitation and decides to engage her in a casual conversation. He shares his own experiences of feeling overwhelmed when he first joined the team. This small exchange helps Jennifer feel more comfortable and valued, illustrating how even a brief interpersonal communication can have a significant impact on relationships and team dynamics.

Human beings are inherently different from each other, and we do not live in isolation. People draw conclusions from our behavior, making communication an integral part of our daily lives. On average, most people spend about 70 to 80% of their waking hours communicating with others. This statistic highlights the significant role communication plays in our lives and its impact on our relationships and overall well-being.

In the human communication model (Figure 4), various types of noise can significantly hinder the clear transmission and reception of messages, making it crucial to recognize and address these barriers.

Physical or External Noise: Includes environmental disturbances such as background music, nearby construction sounds, or conversations in a crowded room that can obscure the intended message and distract both the sender and receiver.

Physiological Noise: Relates to the biological conditions affecting individuals involved in the communication process; this can include hunger, fatigue, illness, or other physical condition that may diminish cognitive clarity and the ability to focus on the conversation at hand.

Psychological Noise Involves the internal mental barriers and emotional states such as biases, prejudices, anxiety, or stress, which can influence how messages are sent, received, and interpreted.

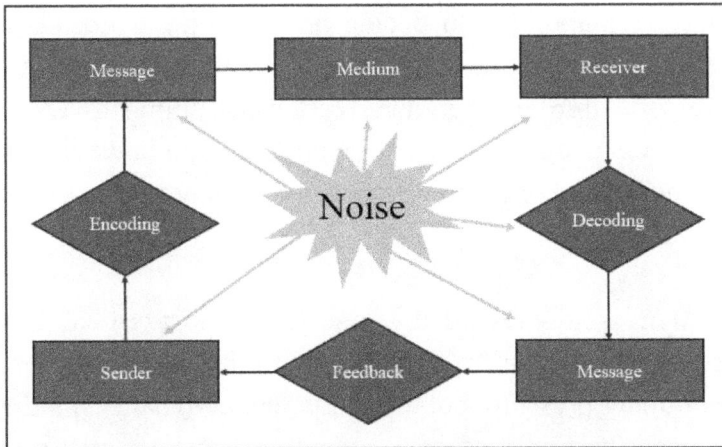

Figure 4. A Model of Human Communication

These internal and external factors can significantly distort communication, leading to misunderstandings and ineffective exchanges, highlighting the importance of minimizing noise for effective communication.

A powerful historical example that underscores the importance of effective interpersonal communication—and the dangers posed by miscommunication or "noise"—occurred during the Cuban Missile Crisis in October 1962, involving the Soviet submarine B-59.

While patrolling near Cuba, B-59 lost contact with Moscow and found itself pursued by U.S. Navy ships, which were dropping non-lethal depth charges intended to force the submarine to surface.

31

However, due to the lack of communication and mounting stress, the crew aboard B-59 believed that war may have already broken out.

In the tense and isolated environment of the submarine, three senior officers were authorized to decide on launching a nuclear-armed T-5 torpedo. Two of the officers gave their consent. But Vasili Arkhipov, the third officer and second-in-command, refused to authorize the launch. He insisted on surfacing and awaiting further instructions instead of escalating what could have led to a full-scale nuclear war.

This moment is now regarded as one of the most critical decisions that prevented nuclear catastrophe—and it hinged not only on judgment under pressure, but on interpersonal dynamics, individual courage, and the profound consequences of unclear or incomplete communication.

Interpersonal communication is governed by several key principles, including:

Governed by rules and ethics: There are prescribed guides that indicate what behavior is obligated, preferred, or prohibited in certain contexts.

Irreversible: Words, once spoken, and messages, once sent, cannot be undone. The irreversible nature of communication demands careful handling, especially in professional settings. A common challenge for many, including seasoned professionals, is the tendency to overreact in face-to-face interactions or in written communications when provoked. Such impulsive reactions can permanently damage relationships and careers.

A stark example is the 2022 Oscars incident, where Will Smith slapped Chris Rock on stage in response to a joke about his wife. This momentary lapse had long-lasting consequences on Smith's reputation and professional opportunities, highlighting the critical importance of managing one's reactions. Learning to control emotional responses is not just advisable—it is imperative. The consequences of failing to do so can be severe and irreversible, as evidenced by individuals who have jeopardized their careers through a single unguarded reaction or a hastily sent email.

Complicated: Communication can fail in many ways. Osmo Wiio, a Scandinavian communication scholar, stated, "If communication can fail, it will. If a message can be understood in different ways, it will be understood in just that way which does the most harm."

Learned/Field of Experience: Communication skills evolve with age and are influenced by a person's culture, past experiences, and personal history.

There are several myths about interpersonal communication that need to be dispelled. One common misconception is that using more words will always make the meaning clearer. In reality, this is not always the case; sometimes, silence can be more powerful and effective than excessive explanation.

Another myth is the belief that information automatically equates to communication. Simply encoding a message does not guarantee that it will be decoded accurately by the recipient. Effective communication requires more than just transmitting information; it involves ensuring that the message is understood as intended.

Finally, there is the assumption that interpersonal relationship problems are always rooted in communication issues. However, this is not necessarily true. People may understand each other perfectly well but still find themselves in disagreement. Communication is just one aspect of relationships, and understanding does not always lead to agreement.

Different communication channels have varying degrees of richness starting with the highest of face-to-face or one-on-one conversation to posted flyer or announcement which is the least effective way of communication.

To be competent in interpersonal communication, one must communicate in ways that are both effective and appropriate. Effective is when the message is understood by others and achieves its intended effects. For example, if you ask someone to wake you up at 5:00 AM, and they do so, your communication was effective. To be appropriate, the communicator should consider the time, place, and overall context of the message and be sensitive to the feelings and attitudes of the listeners.

Effective communication requires focusing on others rather than only on your needs. This includes considering the thoughts and feelings of those you may dislike or who are different from you. It is challenging to communicate effectively when we focus exclusively on ourselves.

Conflict in interpersonal communication can have various negative effects, such as higher stress, reduced morale, and avoidance of the person with whom you have conflict. It may also lead to not contributing your opinions or ideas because you think they will not be heard.

Perception

Perception, from the Latin "perceptio," is the organization, identification, and interpretation of sensory information in order to represent and understand the presented information or the environment. As defined by Schacter Daniel in "Psychology", perception is the process through which we make sense of our surroundings.

Perception is a complex process that goes beyond merely receiving sensory inputs. It involves a sophisticated mechanism where the brain selects, organizes and interprets these inputs to create a coherent understanding of the environment. This process is fundamental to how we interact with the world and each other. The interpretation of sensory information can vary significantly among individuals, influenced by factors such as past experiences, cultural background, and personal biases.

For example, two people might witness the same event but perceive it differently based on their unique perspectives and previous experiences. This variation in perception highlights the subjective nature of reality and the importance of considering multiple viewpoints in interpersonal communication. The media nowadays work on this aspect concerning the information they want to convey based on their position.

Consider the scenario of visiting a location for the first time, carrying preconceived notions informed by a friend's remarks. If you are advised that something unique awaits, you may find yourself dedicating significant effort to uncover this supposed uniqueness, potentially seeing it even in ordinary aspects. Conversely, if you are forewarned about the place's deficiencies, your experience may predominantly involve scrutinizing its shortcomings. This example underscores how our perceptions, molded by prior expectations, can significantly steer our focus and shape our interpretation of experiences.

Consider the Norman Rockwell painting (Figure 5) titled 'Runaway', which appeared on the Saturday Evening Post Cover on September 20, 1958. In the 'Runaway' painting, the scene shows a young boy sitting at a diner counter next to a police officer, with a cook looking on. The interpretation of this scene can vary. Some might see it as a depiction of safety and trust, where the officer is seen as a protector. Others might focus on the boy's feelings, perhaps seeing a sense of adventure or trouble. Such interpretations are shaped by the viewer's own experiences and perceptions of authority figures.

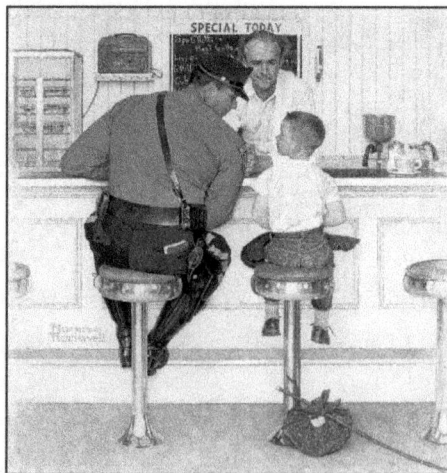

Figure 5. Norman Rockwell Painting

Interpersonal perception involves observing others, as well as interpreting and making judgments about their behavior, intentions, and personalities. This process is continuous and dynamic, as we constantly update our perceptions based on new information and interactions. Understanding the role of perception in interpersonal communication is crucial for building and maintaining effective relationships.

Our five senses—hearing, seeing, smelling, feeling, and tasting—provide the raw data that our brain processes to form perceptions. However, the interpretation of these sensory inputs is influenced by various factors, including attention, memory, and expectations. For example, if you expect someone to be friendly, you are more likely to interpret their actions in a positive manner.

In the selecting stage, we focus on certain stimuli while ignoring others. This selective attention is necessary because our brains cannot process all the sensory information we receive simultaneously. Instead, we filter out irrelevant information and focus on what we consider important. This process is influenced by our needs, interests, and expectations. For example, if you are hungry, you might be more attuned to food-related stimuli.

Selective perception can also lead to biases. For example, if you have a preconceived notion about someone, you might focus on behaviors that confirm your beliefs while ignoring evidence to the contrary. This can reinforce stereotypes and hinder objective judgment.

In the organizing stage, we arrange the selected stimuli into a meaningful pattern. This involves grouping similar items together, distinguishing differences, and forming categories. One common method is superimposing familiar structures onto new information, which helps us make sense of complex data quickly.

For example, when reading a jumbled sentence like 'Yuo cna porbalby raed tihs esaliy desptie teh msispeillgns,' our brains recognize familiar patterns and words, allowing us to understand the message despite the errors.

Punctuation is another organizing principle where we create structure by dividing information into manageable parts. This helps in interpreting the flow and meaning of the message. For example, organizing a series of dots into a recognizable shape or pattern can transform random stimuli into meaningful information.

The interpreting stage involves assigning meaning to the organized stimuli. This stage is highly subjective, as different people can interpret the same stimuli in various ways. Interpretation is influenced by factors such as context, cultural background, and personal experiences.

For example, consider a situation where two friends, Alice and Bob, attend the same event. Alice, who had a positive experience with the speaker in the past, perceives the speaker's message as inspiring. Bob, however, who previously disagreed with the speaker's views, perceives the same message as biased. This scenario demonstrates how past experiences, and personal biases can shape our perception and influence interpersonal communication.

For example, a handshake might be interpreted differently depending on the cultural context—what is considered a friendly gesture in one culture might be seen as inappropriate in another.

Effective interpersonal communication demands an awareness of how our perceptions shape our interactions and a commitment to understanding the perspectives of others. Recognizing the role of perception in interpersonal communication is vital. The way we perceive others influences how we communicate with them, and similarly, their perceptions of us affect how they respond and interact with us.

Carefully manage situations that could be misinterpreted. For example, if someone enters your office loudly complaining about an issue with someone else, it is important to handle this delicately. Onlookers might mistakenly assume the outburst is directed at you, casting both you and the complainer in a potentially negative light. To avoid such misunderstandings, it would be wise to ask the person to return to their office to cool down before discussing the matter further. This approach prevents misperceptions and sets the stage for a more constructive conversation once the person has calmed down.

Barriers to Accurate Perception

Accurate perception is crucial for effective communication, yet several barriers often impede our ability to perceive situations and individuals accurately, leading to misunderstandings and conflicts. By identifying and understanding these barriers, we can take steps to mitigate their effects and enhance our interpersonal interactions:

Ignoring Critical Information: This common barrier occurs when individuals focus only on superficial cues and overlook essential details. This selective attention can lead to hasty judgments based on incomplete or biased information.

Overgeneralizing: This involves judging individuals based on generalized beliefs about a group rather than recognizing their unique characteristics, which can be particularly harmful as it prevents us from seeing people as individuals.

Imposing Consistency: People sometimes fail to notice changes in behavior, continuing to perceive someone based on past impressions. This can obstruct the recognition of growth or changes in the individual.

Focusing on the Negative: There is a common tendency to prioritize negative information over positive. This bias can significantly distort our perceptions and interactions, frequently leading to negative outcomes.

Making Fundamental Attribution Error: This barrier arises when individuals attribute others' behaviors to their character while overlooking situational factors that may influence those behaviors. For instance, someone might be deemed irresponsible for being late, ignoring possible external factors like traffic.

Understanding and addressing these barriers are crucial for enhancing our perception skills and improving interpersonal communication.

Enhancing Perception

Improving perception skills requires conscious effort and practice. One effective strategy is to become more aware of how others perceive you. This involves seeking feedback and being open to criticism. Top athletes, for instance, constantly seek input from their coaches to improve their performance. Similarly, in interpersonal communication, understanding how others perceive us can help us adjust our behavior and improve our interactions.

Increasing your awareness during interactions is another essential step. This can be achieved by focusing on new aspects each time you communicate with someone. For example, paying attention to body language, tone of voice, or emotional cues can provide deeper insights into the person's feelings and intentions.

Becoming other-oriented involves putting yourself in others' shoes to understand their perspectives. This requires empathy and active listening. Understanding the circumstances and backgrounds of others can help in interpreting their behavior more accurately. It also fosters better relationships by showing that you value and respect their viewpoints.

Self-Esteem

Self-esteem refers to the evaluation of our worth or value based on our perceptions of various aspects of ourselves, such as skills, abilities, talents, and appearance. It reflects how we feel about ourselves and our overall sense of self-worth. High self-esteem is characterized by a positive self-assessment, while low self-esteem reflects a more negative view of oneself.

Self-esteem is not synonymous with arrogance or the absence of self-doubt. Individuals with high self-esteem recognize their worth and capabilities without feeling superior to others. They may still experience self-doubt but manage it constructively. For example, others might label someone as lazy, but a person with high self-esteem would not let such judgments define their self-worth.

Building self-esteem is a lifelong process that involves various strategies to enhance one's sense of self-worth. One effective method is engaging in positive self-talk. Intrapersonal communication, or the dialogue we have with ourselves, plays a crucial role in shaping our self-esteem. Positive self-talk involves affirming our strengths and achievements, while negative self-talk tends to focus on our weaknesses and failures. By consciously practicing positive self-talk, we can gradually improve our self-esteem.

Another powerful technique is visualizing a positive image of oneself. For example, if you feel nervous before a meeting, you might imagine everyone in the room congratulating you on your great ideas. This visualization can boost your confidence and help you perform better. The Reticular Activating System (RAS) in our brain, as illustrated in Figure 6, supports this process by filtering incoming information and prioritizing what we deem important. By training our RAS to highlight positive aspects of ourselves, we can reinforce a positive self-image.

The RAS, located in the brainstem, plays a vital role in regulating arousal and consciousness. It acts as a filter for the vast amount of sensory information the brain receives—more than 400 million bits per second. Although the brain is exposed to this massive input, only about 2,000 bits per second reach our conscious awareness, largely due to the RAS's selective filtering function.

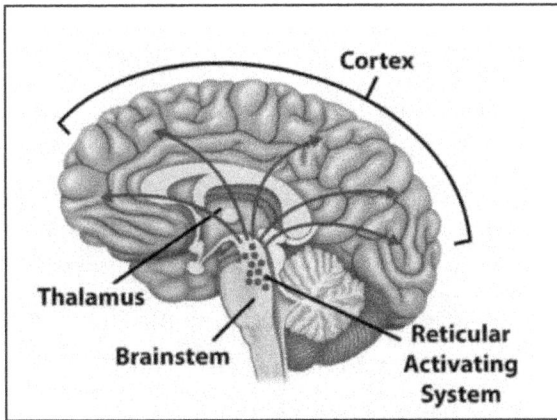

Figure 6. The Reticular Activating System (RAS)

The RAS influences how we perceive the world based on our focus and attention. For instance, if you recently bought a new car, you might suddenly notice many similar cars on the road. This selective attention is directed by the RAS, which highlights information relevant to your recent experiences and interests. Similarly, the RAS can be trained to focus on positive aspects of our lives, thereby enhancing our self-esteem.

The influence of perception and belief on outcomes can be further illustrated by examples from the medical field, such as the placebo effect, sham surgery, and the nocebo effect. The placebo effect occurs when a patient experiences a real improvement in their condition after receiving a treatment that has no therapeutic effect, due to their belief in the treatment's efficacy. Sham surgery involves patients who believe they are undergoing an actual surgical procedure, but no real surgery is performed; minimal or no intervention is used to mimic the process of surgery. Conversely, the nocebo effect occurs when negative expectations about a treatment cause worsening symptoms or new side effects.

In 2023, a significant incident took place when a physician was arrested for charging a patient approximately $20,000 for spine surgery. The patient, placed under anesthesia, after six months discovered that no surgery had been performed, revealing a fraudulent act that underscores the complex interplay of perception, belief, and reality in medical practice.

Self-esteem is crucial for mental health and well-being. It significantly influences our thoughts, emotions, and behaviors. High self-esteem is associated with positive outcomes, such as better stress management, healthier relationships, and greater overall happiness. Conversely, low self-esteem can lead to issues like anxiety, depression, and difficulty in social interactions.

Building and maintaining self-esteem involves developing a realistic and positive self-view. This means acknowledging our achievements and recognizing our potential while being mindful of areas where we can grow. Self-esteem is not static; it fluctuates and can be influenced by various factors, including life events, relationships, and personal achievements. Continuously focusing on self-improvement and self-acceptance is essential for sustaining a healthy level of self-esteem.

Improving Self-Esteem

Improving self-esteem involves several practical steps. One important strategy is to avoid comparing yourself to others. Instead, focus on your positive qualities and work on enhancing your own talents and abilities. Comparisons often lead to feelings of inadequacy and diminish self-esteem.

Developing honest relationships is also vital for building self-esteem. Cultivate friendships with people who can provide genuine feedback and support your personal growth. Having at least one person who can offer objective and honest insights can significantly impact your self-esteem.

Reframing is another effective technique. This involves redefining events and experiences from a different perspective. For example, if you experience a failure, consider it as a learning opportunity rather than a setback. Keeping the larger picture in mind helps in maintaining a balanced view of your self-worth.

The concept of 'fake it till you make it' suggests that acting confident, even when you do not feel it, can eventually lead to genuine confidence. Research supports this idea, indicating that behaviors can influence attitudes and self-perception. By adopting confident behaviors, you might start to internalize those feelings and improve your self-esteem.

Letting go of the past is crucial for building healthy self-esteem. Holding onto past failures or negative experiences can limit your ability to grow and move forward. However, learning from those experiences and choosing to move beyond them empowers you to develop a stronger and more positive self-concept.

A compelling example is Abraham Lincoln, who faced a series of personal and professional setbacks throughout his life. He failed in business multiple times, lost several elections—including bids for the U.S. Senate and Vice Presidency—and endured profound personal losses, such as the death of his fiancée. He also struggled with severe bouts of depression. Yet, Lincoln did not allow these difficulties to define him. Instead, he used them as fuel to persist, ultimately becoming one of the most respected presidents in American history.

Seeking support from professional counselors can also be beneficial. They can help you identify your strengths and work on areas that need improvement. Professional guidance can provide valuable insights and strategies for building self-esteem.

Ultimately, improving self-esteem is an ongoing journey that requires self-awareness, positive thinking, and supportive relationships. By understanding the factors that influence our self-perception and employing strategies to enhance our self-esteem, we can foster better interpersonal communication and lead more fulfilling lives. Remember, the judgments we make about ourselves are the most important, and cultivating a positive self-view is key to personal and professional success.

Active Listening

Hearing is an automatic, physiological process involving the perception of sound waves by the auditory system. It is a passive activity that does not require conscious effort. For example, you might hear the sound of traffic while walking on a busy street without necessarily paying attention to it.

In contrast, listening is an active process that demands concentration and mental engagement. It involves hearing the words, understanding their meanings, interpreting the speaker's intentions, and responding appropriately. Listening is a skill that can be developed and refined with practice.

The distinction between hearing and listening is crucial in interpersonal communication. Effective listening necessitates being present in the moment, free from distractions, and fully engaged with the speaker. This level of engagement is essential for building stronger relationships and fostering mutual understanding.

Active listening is vital in communication, as studies indicate we spend about 45% of our communication time listening, compared to 30% speaking, 15% reading, and 10% writing. This breakdown underscores the importance of developing robust listening skills to enhance overall communication effectiveness.

Further studies reveal that immediately after a 10-minute oral presentation, the average listener has heard, understood, and retained only 50% of what was said. Within 48 hours, this retention drops to about 25%. These statistics show that we often comprehend and retain only a small portion of what we hear, emphasizing the need for strategies to improve retention and comprehension.

Active listening involves more than just hearing words; it requires understanding the underlying messages and emotions conveyed by the speaker. As Jason Wrench explains in 'Stand Up, Speak Out: The Practice and Ethics of Public Speaking', effective listening involves hearing what others say and actively striving to comprehend its meaning.

Consider a scenario involving Lisa, a manager, conducting a meeting with her team. When team member Tom raises a concern about the project's timeline, Lisa, distracted by her phone, only hears part of Tom's concern and responds inadequately, leading to confusion. Upon realizing the miscommunication, Lisa commits to active listening in future meetings. She apologizes to Tom, gives him her full attention, paraphrases his concerns for clarity, and responds thoughtfully. This shift significantly improves communication and trust within the team.

This example illustrates how active listening prevents misunderstandings and fosters a collaborative and respectful work environment.

Listening Barriers

Several barriers can impede effective listening. These barriers can be internal or external and can significantly affect our ability to comprehend and retain information.

Criticizing the Speaker: One common barrier is the tendency to criticize the speaker. Many people get distracted by the speaker's appearance or delivery style, forming impressions based solely on nonverbal information. In addition, disliking the speaker for any reason or past experience can be another barrier. This can prevent effective listening and lead to misunderstandings.

Hot Buttons: Are emotional triggers that elicit immediate, intense reactions. These can include being ignored, encountering bad grammar, or being interrupted. Recognizing and managing these hot buttons is essential for maintaining focus and effective listening.

Differing Speech Rate and Thought Rate: The average person speaks at a rate of about 125 words per minute, but our brains can process information at a much faster rate—around 400 words per minute. This difference means that when we listen to a speaker, we often have mental capacity left over, which can lead to our minds wandering. Making a conscious effort to focus and engage more of our mental capacity on the listening act is crucial.

Age-Related Listening Decline: Studies indicate that our listening skills tend to decline with age. Ralph G. Nichols, a long-time professor of rhetoric, noted that first-grade children are often the best listeners because they give full attention to the speaker. As we age, distractions and preconceived notions can impair our listening abilities.

External Noises: Such as background sounds and environmental distractions, can also impede effective listening. Minimizing these distractions is essential for maintaining focus on the speaker.

Improving Listening Skills

Improving listening skills requires conscious effort and practice. Here are some strategies to enhance listening effectiveness:

Active Listening: This involves fully engaging with the speaker by demonstrating attentive behaviors such as nodding, maintaining appropriate eye contact (while respecting cultural norms), and offering verbal affirmations like "I see" or "Go on." Active listening shows respect for the speaker and fosters an environment conducive to open communication.

Empathetic Listening: Understanding the speaker's feelings and perspectives. It requires putting yourself in the speaker's shoes and responding with empathy and compassion. This type of listening fosters trust and builds stronger interpersonal relationships.

Reflective Listening: Paraphrasing or summarizing the speaker's message to ensure accurate understanding. By reflecting back what the speaker has said, you confirm that you have understood their message correctly and provide an opportunity for clarification if needed.

Critical Listening: Analyzing and evaluating the speaker's message. It requires distinguishing between facts and opinions, identifying biases, and assessing the validity of the information. Critical listening is essential for making informed decisions and developing a well-rounded understanding of the topic.

In summary, active listening is a critical skill for successful interpersonal communication. By understanding the differences between hearing and listening, recognizing and overcoming listening barriers, and employing strategies to improve listening skills, individuals can enhance their ability to communicate effectively. Remember, effective listening involves active engagement, critical thinking, and appropriate feedback.

Non-Verbal Communication

Non-verbal communication encompasses a variety of methods we use to convey messages beyond words. This includes body language, facial expressions, gestures, posture, eye contact, and even the use of space and touch. Often, these non-verbal signals carry more weight and meaning than the spoken words, enriching our interactions with context, emotional depth, and nuanced understanding.

Non-verbal behaviors extend beyond written or spoken language and are pivotal in conveying emotions and attitudes, playing a crucial role in the development of relationships. Psychologist Albert Mehrabian suggests that approximately 93% of the emotional meaning in our messages is communicated non-verbally. This form of communication is essential because it often reveals more honest information about a person's feelings and intentions than verbal expressions.

Consider the interaction between two friends, Emma and Rachel, who reunite after a long separation. Rachel is eager to share some news, but her crossed arms and lack of eye contact signal discomfort. Emma, noticing these cues, pauses to ask if everything is okay, prompting Rachel to share her troubles. This scenario underscores how non-verbal cues can express emotions that words might conceal, fostering deeper understanding and support in relationships.

People tend to control their verbal language to conform to social norms, but non-verbal behaviors are usually more spontaneous and genuine. This authenticity makes non-verbal cues crucial in assessing truthfulness and emotional states. They also enhance the clarity of messages by complementing and reinforcing spoken words.

Non-verbal communication is often deemed more believable than verbal communication because actions can be more telling and harder to falsify. For instance, social psychologists Paul Ekman and Wallace Friesen point out that the face, hands, and feet are key sources of non-verbal cues. Polygraphs, or lie detectors, utilize non-verbal indicators such as blood pressure, pulse, respiration, and skin conductivity to gauge honesty during interrogations.

However, non-verbal messages can be ambiguous, as the sender's intended message may not always match the observer's perception. These messages are also continuous, lacking definite beginnings or endings, which adds complexity to their interpretation.

Cultural differences significantly influence how non-verbal cues are interpreted. A gesture that is considered polite in one culture may be offensive in another. Moreover, non-verbal cues often occur simultaneously across different channels, requiring observers to integrate multiple signals to decode the intended message accurately.

Non-Verbal Communication Codes

Non-verbal communication encompasses various codes that play distinct roles in conveying meaning beyond words. These codes include facial expressions, vocal cues, personal space, touch, and appearance.

Each code delivers unique types of information and can vary greatly depending on context and individual differences. Gaining an understanding of these codes is essential for decoding the rich tapestry of non-verbal communication.

Facial Expressions

Are a primary method of non-verbal communication, capable of conveying a wide range of emotions quickly and effectively. The human face can produce a vast number of expressions, serving as a dynamic tool for non-verbal exchange.

Accurately recognizing and interpreting these expressions is key to understanding others' emotional states and intentions. For instance, surprise might be shown by wide-open eyes and a raised brow, whereas fear might include an open mouth and tense skin under the eyes.

Vocal Cues

Encompass more than just words; they include tone, pitch, volume, and speaking rate. These elements can dramatically alter the meaning of a spoken message. Sarcasm, for example, is often conveyed more through tone than the actual words used. Attuning to these vocal cues offers deeper insights into a speaker's true feelings and attitudes, such as excitement indicated by a higher pitch or thoughtfulness suggested by a slower rate.

A notable application of understanding vocal cues is the 'WhyCry' device, developed by a Spanish engineer. This device interprets a baby's cries, indicating hunger, sleepiness, or stress, demonstrating the capability of vocal analysis in decoding non-verbal communication.

Personal Space

The concept of personal space varies across cultures and contexts and is essential for avoiding misunderstandings in social interactions. It encompasses both physical distance and psychological boundaries. Understanding and respecting these boundaries are crucial for maintaining harmonious relationships. Edward Hall's study of proxemics highlights four zones: intimate, personal, social, and public, each defining a different level of closeness or formality.

Touch
Is a powerful form of non-verbal communication that can convey a wide range of emotions—from reassurance and support to discomfort or rejection. Its meaning varies greatly depending on the context, type, frequency, and the nature of the relationship between individuals. In professional environments, touch may be used to express authority, encouragement, or solidarity. However, it is essential that any physical contact remains within the boundaries of cultural norms and expectations to avoid misinterpretation or discomfort.

Appearance
Including attire, grooming, and overall presentation, plays a significant role in shaping how others perceive us. It can influence first impressions, credibility, and attraction. Dressing professionally might convey competence, while casual attire might suggest friendliness and approachability.

Enhancing Non-Verbal Communication Skills
Improving your ability to interpret non-verbal communication requires a combination of keen observation, cultural sensitivity, and ongoing feedback. Actively observing the full spectrum of non-verbal cues and understanding their context can significantly enhance interpersonal interactions.

Active Observation: This involves paying close attention to both the obvious cues, such as facial expressions and gestures, and subtler signs, including interpersonal distance, posture, and paralinguistic cues like tone and pitch of voice.

For instance, consider a meeting where a colleague verbally expresses agreement with a plan, yet displays contradictory non-verbal cues: their arms are crossed and their voice lacks inflection. Such behaviors might suggest reluctance or disagreement despite their spoken words. It's crucial to observe these cues in clusters rather than in isolation, as this approach allows for more accurate interpretations of the colleague's true feelings and intentions.

Cultural Awareness: Non-verbal communication is heavily influenced by cultural norms. For example, in some cultures, direct eye contact is seen as a sign of confidence and honesty, while in others, it may be perceived as disrespectful or confrontational. Developing an understanding of these cultural nuances is crucial, especially in international or multicultural settings.

A helpful approach is to research or ask about appropriate non-verbal behavior before entering a new cultural environment to avoid miscommunication. For example, a businessperson from the U.S. working in Japan might learn that bowing, rather than shaking hands, is a common non-verbal greeting and sign of respect.

Seeking and Giving Feedback: Feedback is essential for understanding how well one's non-verbal communication is perceived by others. It can be beneficial to ask close colleagues, friends, or mentors to provide feedback on your non-verbal behavior. This feedback can reveal habitual patterns, such as restlessness during presentations or maintaining poor eye contact during conversations, which you might not be aware of.

Conversely, offering gentle, constructive feedback to others about their non-verbal communication can help strengthen mutual understanding and improve team dynamics.

Practicing Empathy: Being empathetic helps in interpreting non-verbal cues more effectively. It involves putting yourself in the other person's shoes and trying to understand their emotional state or perspective.

For example, noticing that a team member appears unusually quiet and withdrawn could prompt a manager to privately inquire if they need support, rather than ignoring their behavior or pushing them to participate more actively.

By focusing on these aspects of non-verbal communication and continuously practicing these skills, individuals can become more adept at navigating complex interpersonal situations and building stronger, more effective relationships.

Summary

Interpersonal communication is a complex and dynamic process that is vital in shaping our relationships, self-esteem, and overall well-being. Through both verbal and non-verbal interactions, we exchange information and express emotions, intentions, and perceptions that significantly influence our connections with others.

Grasping the principles and complexities of interpersonal communication—such as the effects of perception, the critical role of active listening, and the subtleties of non-verbal cues—enables us to navigate through social interactions more effectively. By recognizing and addressing barriers to accurate perception and listening, we enhance our ability to communicate with clarity and empathy.

Furthermore, our self-esteem is crucial in how we present ourselves and engage with others. Cultivating a positive self-view and committing to self-improvement can significantly enhance both our personal and professional relationships. The capabilities to listen actively, perceive accurately, and respond thoughtfully are fundamental in forming strong, meaningful connections that foster a supportive and cooperative environment.

Ultimately, the success of our interpersonal communication relies on our continuous awareness and adaptability. By consistently refining our communication skills, we can deepen our understanding of others, articulate ourselves more effectively, and foster more satisfying relationships. Interpersonal communication transcends mere word exchange; it involves building a shared understanding that strengthens our bonds and enriches our collective experiences.

Chapter Three

Organizational Culture: Living the Values

O rganizational culture encompasses a complex web of shared values, beliefs, and practices that dictate how individuals within a company interact and collaborate to achieve common goals. This culture forms the backbone of any organization, significantly impacting its atmosphere and the overall job satisfaction of its employees. Beyond influencing daily interactions and decision-making processes, organizational culture shapes the strategic direction and long-term viability of a company.

Throughout this chapter, we will explore the dynamics of organizational culture, examining how it shapes individual and collective behaviors and plays a crucial role in embedding the organization's values and advancing its achievements. We will also look at practical examples of how different organizations apply these concepts to foster environments where both the company and its employees can thrive.

Organizational Culture

As Herb Kelleher, the celebrated CEO of Southwest Airlines, famously emphasized, culture should take precedence over other business aspects. Organizational culture, at its essence, consists of the shared beliefs and values that define a company's identity. These values, which are stable over time, provide a framework that guides employees' actions and decision-making processes. Yet, despite its deep-rooted nature, organizational culture is not static; it evolves, albeit slowly, reflecting the dynamic nature of the businesses themselves.

New employees, with their fresh perspectives, are particularly adept at discerning the prevailing cultural dynamics, which long-term employees might overlook. These newcomers can identify whether stated values like collaboration are genuinely embraced or merely listed in corporate literature. This phase of observation is crucial, as it can reveal discrepancies between the organization's espoused values and the values enacted by its employees.

Statistical Insights on Organizational Culture

The alignment between espoused and enacted values has a quantifiable impact on recruitment, retention, and overall organizational health, as evidenced by the following statistics from Kate Heinz's analysis in her article, "42 Shocking Company Culture Statistics You Need to Know" (originally published in 2019 and updated in 2022):

- 15% have declined job offers due to incompatible company culture.

- 24% increase in likelihood of quitting among employees dissatisfied with their company's culture.

- 33% of job seekers would accept a 10% pay cut for a job they are passionate about.

- 58% would prefer a lower-paying job if it meant working for a great boss.

- 88% believe that strong company culture is essential for business success.

These statistics highlight the importance of a positive organizational culture in attracting and retaining talent, reducing turnover, and enhancing job satisfaction.

Whenever colleagues and friends approached me for advice after receiving job offers with higher pay than their current positions, I always advised them to consider the entire package, not just the salary. Sometimes a person may be fortunate to receive a financially better offer, but it is essential to evaluate other factors such as the company culture, management style, work environment, teamwork, and job stability. These elements are critical in determining the true value of a job offer and can significantly impact one's satisfaction and growth within a company.

Management's Role in Cultivating Culture

Management plays a pivotal role in shaping and maintaining the cultural foundation of an organization. Managers who truly embody and uphold the company's values create an environment where employees feel valued and understood, which enhances loyalty and reduces turnover. A strong organizational culture, supported by effective leadership, retains talent and attracts new candidates, particularly in competitive job markets.

However, not everyone is naturally suited for a supervisory, management, or leadership role, and recognizing this is crucial for the health of an organization. Leadership requires a unique set of skills, such as emotional intelligence, the ability to manage people effectively, and the capacity to make sound decisions under pressure. While some individuals excel as contributors or specialists, they may lack the necessary traits or desire to lead. It is important for management to respect the choices of employees who prefer to remain as contributors rather than stepping into leadership roles. Many employees find greater fulfillment and passion in specialized or individual contributor roles, and recognizing and honoring this preference is crucial to maintaining their engagement and morale.

Unfortunately, many organizations promote employees based solely on performance or tenure, without adequately assessing their readiness for people management. This often results in individuals being promoted to roles they are not equipped for, leading to inefficiency and frustration for both the employee and their team. It is essential that employees are fully prepared and equipped for the next level before being promoted. This includes providing training, mentorship, and development opportunities to cultivate the skills necessary for effective management. When employees are promoted based on their readiness, rather than solely on seniorities, the organization benefits from a more cohesive, motivated, and productive workforce.

Trust and integrity in management are essential for maintaining a healthy organizational culture. Once trust is broken, it can be incredibly difficult to rebuild, and the damage can severely undermine leadership credibility. If employees perceive management as dishonest or unreliable, it erodes trust and weakens the overall foundation of the workplace. Rebuilding trust, once broken, is a lengthy and challenging process.

While management must demonstrate consistency and transparency, employees also share responsibility in maintaining trust. Some employees, for example, misuse privileges like sick leave, treating them as an entitlement even when they are not genuinely ill. During the COVID-19 pandemic, many companies faced challenges as some employees abused the working remotely policy, which led to decreased engagement and lower productivity. These actions damage trust, undermine accountability, and erode morale. A healthy workplace culture depends on mutual trust, respect, and accountability from both management and employees.

I have also witnessed firsthand how a breakdown in trust can persist over time. In a new management role at a company I worked for few years ago, one of the managers who reported directly to me—not just a regular employee—came to ask for permission to leave early for his child's birthday. To my surprise, he brought along his child's birth certificate as proof. This gesture revealed a deeper issue, suggesting lingering mistrust from previous management. It was unclear whether this mistrust originated from that manager's side or from previous leadership, but it was clear that there was a trust issue somewhere.

Additionally, I have observed managers who claim to treat everyone equally and uphold fairness, maintaining an equal distance from all employees—using the analogy of a ruler to measure uniformity. However, over time, their actions resemble more of a protractor, with the distance shifting based on personal closeness to certain employees, favoritism, or hidden agendas. Such inconsistency breeds frustration and gradually erodes the essential trust between management and staff.

Reflecting on the maxim, "People do not care how much you know until they know how much you care," highlights the importance of emotional intelligence and genuine concern in leadership. Employees tend to value the human side of their leaders—empathy, sincerity, and care—far more than professional credentials, position, or education. This reinforces the idea that effective leadership is built on personal connection as much as competence and authority.

Companies like Google, Zappos, and Patagonia exemplify the impact of strong organizational cultures. Google fosters an innovative and flexible work environment through initiatives like '20% projects,' encouraging creativity and autonomy. Zappos promotes cultural fit by offering new hires a financial incentive to leave if they feel the culture is not right for them. Patagonia lives its values of sustainability by supporting employees in environmental volunteerism. These examples illustrate that organizational culture goes beyond written values in handbooks; it is reflected in daily practices and policies that reinforce those values.

Investing in a robust organizational culture and competent leadership is critical for any company aiming for long-term success in today's competitive business environment. These efforts help to reduce employee turnover, boost job satisfaction, and provide a competitive edge in recruitment, all of which contribute to the organization's enduring success.

Characteristics of Organizational Culture

Organizational culture is more than just the visible symbols and rituals; it is deeply ingrained in the fabric of the company. It is passed on to new employees through socialization processes and influences behavior at work. Artifacts, like logos and uniforms, are easier to change, but the less visible aspects of culture, such as values and assumptions, are more resistant to alteration. These characteristics make organizational culture a powerful force in shaping how employees interact and perform their duties.

Schein's Model of Organizational Culture

The iceberg diagram in Figure 7 provides a vivid illustration of Edgar Schein's Model of Organizational Culture, effectively breaking down the complex concept of organizational culture into three distinct, integral layers.

This model, developed by Edgar Schein, helps in understanding how culture functions within organizations by differentiating between the visible and invisible forces at play. The diagram uses the metaphor of an iceberg to symbolize the layered nature of culture, where many remain hidden beneath the surface.

By exploring these layers—ranging from the most overt and observable elements to the deeply embedded, unconscious beliefs—

Schein's Model offers a comprehensive framework for analyzing the dynamics that shape organizational behavior and performance.

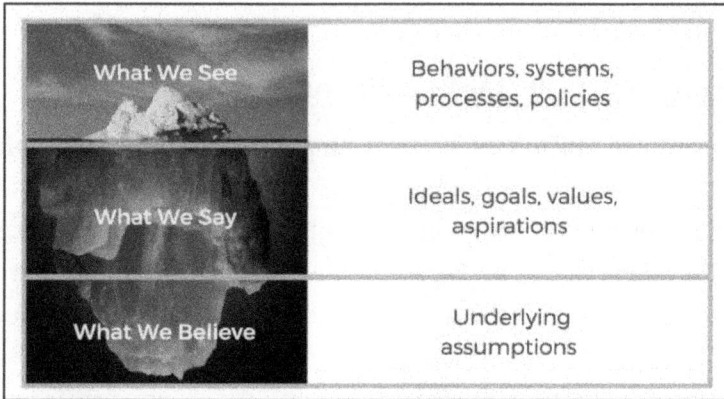

What We See	Behaviors, systems, processes, policies
What We Say	Ideals, goals, values, aspirations
What We Believe	Underlying assumptions

Figure 7. Schein's Model of Organizational Culture

Artifacts (What We See): This visible layer includes all tangible and overt elements such as a company's physical environment, attire regulations, and public communications. Artifacts are the most easily discernible aspects of organizational culture.

Example: A corporation prominently features an open-plan office layout and modern design to symbolize transparency and encourage collaboration among employees.

Espoused Values (What We Say): This intermediate layer encapsulates the declared principles and standards that the organization publicly endorses, which include its mission statements, goals, and ethical codes.

Example: A financial institution asserts its commitment to ethical banking and responsibility in its marketing materials and internal policies, promoting integrity as a core company value.

Underlying Assumptions (What We Believe): The deepest layer, these are the subconscious beliefs and assumptions that are rarely articulated but critically shape organizational behaviors and attitudes. These foundational beliefs are the true drivers of an organization's culture.

Example: Even though a company may claim to value work-life balance, there might be an unspoken assumption that staying late at the office is a sign of greater commitment and the key to promotion, subtly influencing employee behavior.

Toxic Workplace Culture

A toxic workplace culture can profoundly undermine employee morale, organizational performance, and long-term sustainability. Recognizing the indicators of such a culture is essential to initiating corrective actions that mitigate its detrimental effects. These indicators often manifest as shifts in team dynamics, heightened work-related stress, growing employee disengagement, and increased turnover rates.

Warning signs—such as reduced collaboration, escalating conflicts, and limited opportunities for professional growth—are indicative of a work environment that negatively impacts both individual employees and the organization as a whole.

A common example of how organizations respond to toxic workplace cultures is the implementation of rigid attendance-monitoring systems, such as fingerprint scanners, to enforce punctuality. These systems are often introduced not because they are the most effective solution, but because management lacks either the authority or the willingness to directly address employees who repeatedly violate attendance expectations. Consequently, the system is applied across the board, effectively penalizing the entire team for the behavior of a few. While such measures may ensure physical presence, they often fail to foster mental or emotional engagement. In fact, employees may find ways to bypass or manipulate the system, which only serves to erode trust and morale even further.

External awards and media recognition can sometimes present a distorted image of success for companies or individuals, concealing underlying internal challenges. While organizations may enjoy the prestige of public accolades, these honors often overshadow the realities of their internal culture and operational struggles. True success arises from genuinely earned ethical practices and meaningful actions, not from superficial recognition. Ultimately, the true measure of a company's culture is found in the daily actions, attitudes, and behaviors of its employees, not in awards or media coverage.

The well-known Enron scandal stands as a powerful example of how a toxic organizational culture can undermine even the most celebrated companies. For those unfamiliar, Enron was a U.S.-based energy company once hailed for its innovation, aggressive growth, and market leadership. It was widely praised by investors, analysts, and the media—earning numerous awards and accolades.

However, behind this polished image, Enron fostered a deeply flawed internal culture marked by unethical behavior, excessive risk-taking, and a severe lack of transparency and accountability. This disconnect between external reputation and internal reality ultimately led to one of the largest corporate collapses in history.

The Enron case highlights the dangerous consequences of ignoring cultural health, showing that public acclaim cannot compensate for a corrosive work environment.

For an organization to thrive, early identification and elimination of toxic elements within its culture are crucial. This process requires fostering open communication, promoting ethical behavior, and ensuring that all employees feel valued and supported. Importantly, employees at all levels should have direct access to someone in executive management who listens to them. This access is particularly vital when issues stem from direct supervisors, as these problems can be misrepresented or fail to reach senior leadership.

A lack of clear communication can obscure the true nature of issues, hindering executives from fully understanding and addressing underlying problems. In one instance during my career, our team spent an entire year working diligently to bypass a senior direct manager and escalate an issue directly to executive management, as the senior manager was the source of the problem.

This situation highlights the necessity for higher-up managers to maintain open lines of communication with employees at all levels. Doing so leads to better outcomes and significantly enhances the work culture, helping to prevent toxic organizational environments.

While writing this book, I visited a customer service office for some work, where the front desk representative quickly began voicing frustration with the company's management and workplace culture. He even admitted to actively seeking opportunities elsewhere. This was not an isolated incident; a few years earlier, I had heard similar concerns from another employee at the same company. Although management might take comfort in the company's operational success, neglecting employee satisfaction is clearly eroding the culture, undermining morale, and jeopardizing the organization's long-term resilience.

Swiftly addressing these issues is critical, as unaddressed toxic behaviors risk becoming deeply entrenched, making meaningful change increasingly difficult. By proactively confronting toxic behaviors early, organizations can prevent harmful practices from becoming normalized. This approach cultivates a healthy, productive workplace and ensures that employees remain engaged and empowered, ultimately contributing to the organization's long-term success.

Personal Values

Personal values serve as the bedrock of our actions and choices, shaping our behavior and guiding our decision-making processes from a young age. These values are deeply influenced by cultural backgrounds, family dynamics, and personal experiences, forming a framework through which we view and interact with the world.

In a corporate environment, it is essential to align these personal values with the values upheld by the organization, as this alignment is crucial for achieving both personal fulfillment and enhancing organizational performance.

This section explores deeper into the significance of personal values, emphasizing their role in developing self-awareness, guiding behavior, and the critical importance of aligning them with an organization's values.

Personal values are the convictions and ethical standards we hold dearly, guiding us in discerning what is right and essential. They influence how we interact with others and make decisions, serving as a personal compass. While many of these values are instilled during childhood through family norms and cultural teachings, they are also shaped and refined by our ongoing personal experiences and the various environments we navigate.

As individuals progress to school, the educational system can further these leadership traits by fostering an environment that emphasizes mutual respect and the development of leadership skills. Schools can implement programs that promote leadership roles among students in various activities, encouraging them to take initiative, manage projects, and lead teams. This experience is invaluable, as it provides young leaders with practical skills in managing both tasks and people.

The journey continues at the college level, where students are given the autonomy to choose their majors and explore subjects that align with their interests and values. Colleges can support this by providing a flexible curriculum that encourages students to take leadership roles in group projects and student organizations. Here, the focus is on enhancing their leadership capabilities through practical application and critical thinking, preparing them for real-world challenges.

When these individuals enter the workforce, they bring the necessary academic knowledge along with the leadership competencies essential for career advancement. Employers can capitalize on this by offering ongoing leadership development programs that refine these skills and prepare individuals for higher managerial roles, ensuring that they can apply their values in ways that propel both their personal growth and the organization's objectives.

It is important to recognize that it is never too late to establish or redefine one's personal values. Even as professionals, setting core values is crucial for defining one's identity and guiding behavior in both personal and professional domains. These values reflect who we are and shape our interactions, decisions, and path to success.

Defining Personal Values

For many, identifying and committing to a few core personal values can be a challenging yet enlightening process. It involves deep introspection and an understanding of what truly matters to oneself. One practical approach to defining personal values is to start with a broader list of values that resonate with you. This list might initially include as many as ten values that you feel are important. Over time, through experiences and reflection, this list can be refined to five or six core values. This refinement process helps in focusing on what is most essential, not implying that other values are unimportant but rather highlighting those that are most influential in your personal and professional life.

Defining these core values is more than an exercise in identification; it is about integrating these values into your daily life and letting them guide your actions and decisions. For instance, if integrity is a core value, this should be evident in your dealings with colleagues, in your commitment to honesty in your work, and in how you handle ethical dilemmas. Similarly, if innovation is a value, it should drive you to seek continuous improvement and creative solutions in your field.

Moreover, setting personal values can be a dynamic process. As individuals grow and experience new challenges, their values can evolve. What was important in one's twenties may shift as they enter different phases of their career and life. This evolution reflects personal growth and adaptation, which are both natural and necessary for long-term success and fulfillment.

In essence, defining and refining personal values is a vital ongoing process that shapes both professional identities and personal lives. By clearly understanding and adhering to these values, individuals can maintain a consistent and authentic approach to life and work, paving the way for genuine fulfillment and success in their endeavors. This approach ensures that one's actions and decisions align with their deepest beliefs and aspirations, creating a strong foundation for both personal integrity and professional excellence.

The Barrett Model of Personal Values

The Barrett Model outlines seven areas in the development and growth of personal awareness, emphasizing the spectrum of human motivation (Figure 8). These areas are divided into three main categories: Self-Interest, Transformation, and the Common Good.

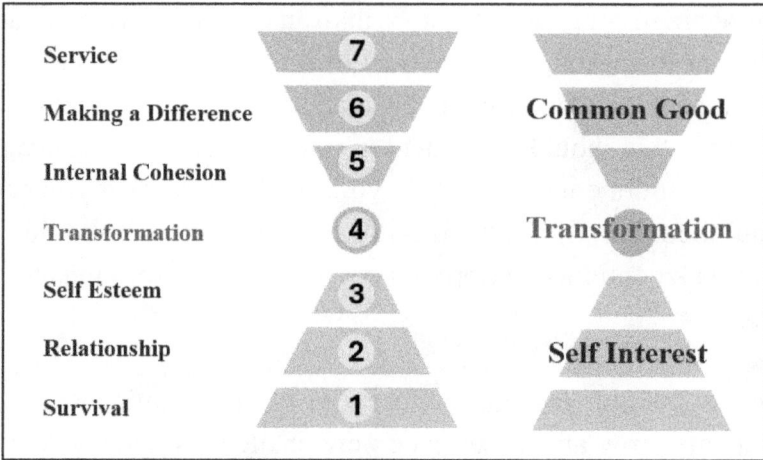

Figure 8. The Barrett Model of Personal Values

Self-Interest: Examples of values in the Self-Interest category include the need for financial security, which is represented by behaviors such as saving money or seeking stable employment. Another example is the value of social recognition, which motivates individuals to seek validation and approval from others. The need for personal safety can drive behaviors such as risk aversion and cautious decision-making.

Transformation: In the Transformation category, examples of values include the pursuit of personal growth, where individuals focus on self-improvement and learning. The value of autonomy is another example, driving individuals to seek independence and control over their own lives. The desire for meaningful work reflects a value that motivates individuals to find purpose in their professional lives.

Common Good: The Common Good category is characterized by values that prioritize the well-being of others and the broader community. These values include a commitment to social responsibility, where individuals seek to contribute positively to society. Selflessness, for example, motivates actions that benefit others without expecting anything in return. Environmental stewardship is another value in this category, where individuals take actions that protect and preserve the natural world for future generations. The focus in this category shifts from personal gains to the collective good, emphasizing the importance of contributing to the welfare of others and society as a whole.

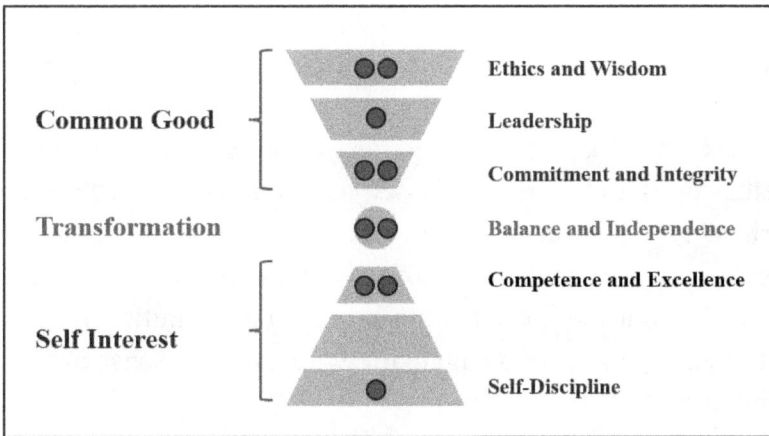

Figure 9. A Sample of Barrett Model

The sample of the Barrett Model shown above (Figure 9) demonstrates a balanced distribution across the three core areas of the model: Self-Interest, Transformation, and Common Good. Such a distribution indicates that the individual possesses a well-rounded range of values, encompassing basic survival needs, personal growth aspirations, and a commitment to societal welfare. This comprehensive approach highlights the individual's capacity to integrate personal development with contributions to the broader

75

community, effectively embodying the ideals proposed by the Barrett Model in a real-world context.

The Importance of Personal Values

Personal values are fundamental to defining who we are and how we interact with the world. These values shape our behavior, influence our attitudes, and guide our responses to various situations, both in personal and professional contexts. As such, they play a critical role in our overall well-being and success.

Guiding Daily Behavior and Attitudes: At the core, personal values are the principles and standards we hold dear, acting as compasses that guide our actions, decisions, and interactions. Whether consciously or subconsciously, our values determine our priorities and provide a framework for understanding the world around us. They influence how we perceive our roles in our workplaces, our families, and our broader communities. By staying true to these values, we navigate life with a clearer sense of purpose and integrity.

Enhancing Motivation and Focus: Personal values are also instrumental in driving our motivation and maintaining our focus. When we engage in activities or works that align with our values, we are naturally more passionate and dedicated. For example, someone who values creativity will find deep satisfaction in a role that allows them to innovate and express themselves, thereby staying motivated even in the face of challenges. Similarly, someone who values helping others will feel more fulfilled working in service-oriented professions or in roles that impact the well-being of others.

Fostering Personal and Professional Fulfillment: Aligning personal actions with personal values enhances job satisfaction and contributes to a sense of personal fulfillment. When our careers and daily activities reflect our values, we experience a greater harmony and contentment in life. This alignment reduces internal conflicts that can occur when living in contradiction to one's principles, which is crucial for maintaining mental and emotional well-being.

Aiding Decision-Making: Moreover, personal values serve as critical benchmarks for decision-making. When faced with choices, big or small, referring back to our values can provide clarity and direction. This can be particularly valuable in complex or high-pressure situations where the right course of action is not immediately apparent. By asking whether a potential decision aligns with our values, we can choose paths that are effective, ethically sound, and personally satisfying.

Providing a Sense of Purpose and Direction: Beyond guiding everyday decisions and behaviors, personal values infuse our lives with a sense of purpose and direction. They help us define our goals and aspirations and shape our understanding of success. Values such as justice, community, integrity, and innovation can inspire individuals to pursue careers and personal paths that bring both personal fulfillment and contribute to the greater good.

Recently, I listened to an interview with an employee who held a diplomatic position for many years—a role that many would consider a dream job. However, she ultimately chose to resign because following certain directives would have conflicted with her core values. Reflecting on her decision, she described it as "devastating," explaining, "This job was not just work; it was my identity. I felt an immense pride in what I was doing." After leaving, she expressed a sense of relief, and when asked if she regretted her decision, her response was striking: "No, absolutely not. I do not regret it at all. In fact, I am grateful that I had the ability to resign. At the deepest levels—morally, humanly, legally—my soul simply would not let me stay in this career. I believe we have one life, and I need to make the most of the life I have been given." Reaching this level of conviction provides a powerful example of what it truly means to live by one's values.

It is worth noting that two of the most essential personal values every individual should embody in their life are strength and integrity. Strength is not limited to knowledge, learning, or taking on responsibility; it also encompasses standing up for what is right and defending it to uphold principles of justice and fairness. Integrity, on the other hand, is about maintaining trust and safeguarding what one is entrusted with, whether it involves workplace confidentiality or other responsibilities, in alignment with one's conscience and ethical values.

In essence, personal values are far more than abstract ideas; they are practical, powerful guides that enrich every dimension of our lives. They keep us grounded, enable wise and consistent choices, drive us toward genuine passions, and empower us to live authentically. Cultivating and adhering to a well-defined set of personal values is essential for anyone striving to lead a meaningful and impactful life.

Corporate Values

Corporate values are the fundamental beliefs and principles that guide a company's actions, decisions, and behaviors. These values form the cornerstone of the organizational culture (Figure 10), influencing how employees interact with one another and with external stakeholders.

A strong set of corporate values drives ethical behavior and helps build a cohesive, productive work environment. In this section, we explore the importance of corporate values, the gap between espoused values—the values a company claims to uphold—and enacted values—the values that are actually practiced by employees, and the role these values play in shaping an organization's identity and success.

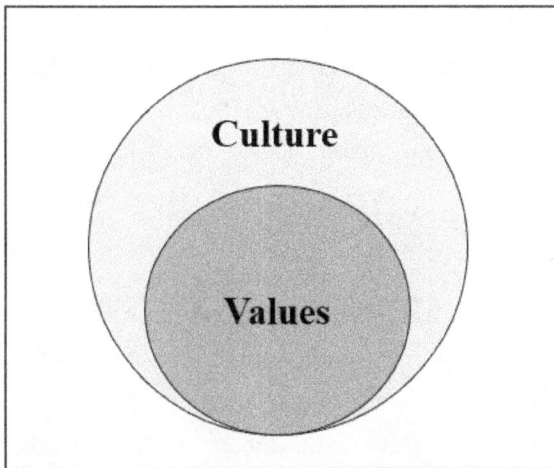

Figure 10. Values-Culture Relationship

A key challenge in maintaining a strong organizational culture is ensuring alignment between espoused and enacted values. Discrepancies between these two can lead to confusion, frustration, and a loss of credibility among employees and external stakeholders.

79

For example, a company might profess a commitment to sustainability, an increasingly common value among modern businesses. However, if the company's operations continue to significantly harm the environment, or if it fails to invest in sustainable practices and technologies, the actual values (enacted) contradict what is claimed (espoused). This discrepancy not only undermines the company's efforts to foster a cohesive and genuine culture but can also lead to disillusionment and turnover among employees who value environmental responsibility.

Such gaps are detrimental both internally and externally, as they can impact the organization's reputation and its relationships with customers, partners, and the broader community. Addressing these discrepancies is crucial for maintaining organizational integrity and achieving long-term success.

The Role of Corporate Values

Corporate values serve as the foundation of an organization's culture. They define what the company stands for and influence every aspect of its operations. Values such as integrity, innovation, and respect for individuals are often emphasized to convey business professionalism and ethical standards. These values are not just abstract concepts; they are the basic core of conduct that guides employees in their daily activities and decision-making processes. A company that clearly articulates and lives by its values is more likely to foster trust, loyalty, and a strong sense of purpose among its employees.

To further understand the impact of corporate values, consider the case study of Ritz-Carlton and McDonald's. Ritz-Carlton's culture is built on a foundation of service excellence, where every employee is empowered to create memorable experiences for guests. In contrast, McDonald's emphasizes efficiency and consistency, focusing on delivering a uniform product and experience across its global operations. These examples illustrate how corporate values shape both the internal culture and the external perception of the brand.

The Impact of Corporate Values on Organizational Success

The importance of corporate values extends beyond shaping internal culture; they also play a crucial role in determining organizational success. Research has shown that companies with strong, adaptive cultures tend to perform better financially and are more resilient in the face of challenges. For instance, mergers and acquisitions often fail due to incompatible corporate cultures, highlighting the significance of aligning values during such transitions.

Moreover, companies that prioritize succession planning by reinforcing their corporate values are better equipped to ensure continuity in leadership and strategic management.

Several companies have demonstrated the power of living their corporate values. For example, Marriott emphasizes 'passionate attitudes at all levels,' ensuring that every employee, regardless of their position, contributes to the organization's success.

Another example is the NASA janitor who famously said, "I am helping put a man on the moon," illustrating how even those in seemingly minor roles can fully embrace and embody the organization's mission and values. This story serves as a powerful reminder not to underestimate the importance of our work, regardless of our role. It is crucial to see our contributions as integral to the bigger picture, advancing the organization's strategic goals.

Organizational Socialization and the Transmission of Values

Organizational socialization is the process through which new employees learn and internalize the values, norms, and behaviors required to function effectively within the organization. This process begins even before an individual joins the company, during the anticipatory socialization phase, where they form expectations based on the information available about the organization. Once onboard, employees go through the encounter phase, where they experience the organization's culture firsthand. The first few months are critical in this process, as new hires learn to navigate the realities of their workplace and reconcile any discrepancies between their expectations and actual experiences.

This highlights the importance of the probation period typically found in some employment contracts, which provides both the employee and the employer with an agreed-upon timeframe to evaluate their professional relationship in practice. During this period, either party has the right to terminate the contract without any additional obligations or the need to disclose reasons.

The Ethical Dimension of Corporate Values

Ethics are the foundation upon which corporate values are built, serving as the guiding principles that influence every decision and action within an organization. A strong ethical framework within an organization promotes trust, integrity, and accountability while also setting the tone for the entire corporate culture.

Companies that prioritize ethical behavior are better positioned to build long-term, trusting relationships with their stakeholders, including employees, customers, and partners, and to avoid the pitfalls of legal and reputational risks.

The Interplay Between Personal, Corporate, and Cultural Values

Ethical behavior in the workplace is not merely the result of a company's policies but is deeply influenced by the interplay between an individual's personal values, the corporate values they are expected to uphold, and the broader cultural values within which they operate. When these three sets of values align, individuals are more likely to make decisions that reflect both personal integrity and organizational ethics. However, when there is a misalignment, ethical dilemmas can arise, requiring individuals to navigate complex situations where their personal values may be at odds with corporate or cultural expectations.

Consider the story of Sarah, a mid-level manager at a large pharmaceutical company known for its commitment to innovation and patient care. Sarah has always held personal values of honesty, transparency, and social responsibility, which align well with her company's stated corporate values. The company promotes a culture of putting patient welfare above all else, which is echoed in its marketing and public communications.

One day, Sarah is asked to review the data from a clinical trial for a new drug that the company plans to bring to market. As she reviews the data carefully, she discovers that while the drug shows promise, there are some serious side effects that have not been fully disclosed in the summary reports provided to the senior management team. The corporate culture within her department, however, is one of aggressive growth and rapid product development, where the pressure to meet deadlines and launch new products is intense.

Sarah faces an ethical dilemma: Should she raise concerns about the side effects, knowing it could delay the product launch and possibly harm her career prospects? Or should she remain silent and allow the drug to proceed, potentially putting patients at risk but aligning with the aggressive corporate culture of meeting targets and driving profitability?

The challenge lies in the fact that yielding one's values even a single time under pressure can lead to easier compromises in the future, thereby progressively undermining personal integrity. As time progresses, individuals might find themselves trapped by their previous actions, which could potentially be used for coercion or blackmail in later situations. Moreover, if unlawful activities connected to these compromises are exposed within a group the individual belongs to, they could be made a scapegoat and face allegations based on their former conduct. Consequently, steadfast adherence to personal values is essential to sidestep these dangers and to safeguard one's reputation and professional dignity.

Sarah's personal values of honesty and responsibility compel her to act. She decides to bring the issue to the attention of her superiors, despite the potential backlash. Her decision is driven by her belief that patient safety should come before profit, a belief that aligns with the company's espoused corporate values yet contradicts the unspoken, high-pressure culture within her department.

Sarah's actions led to an internal investigation, and while the product launch is delayed, the company eventually releases a safer drug with full transparency about the risks. Her courage in standing by her personal and ethical principles earns her the respect of senior management, and over time, the company begins to shift its internal culture to better align with its corporate values, reducing the emphasis on speed at the expense of safety.

This example illustrates how the alignment—or misalignment—of personal values, corporate values, and cultural norms can shape an individual's response to ethical situations. When employees feel supported in making ethical decisions that align with their personal values and the company's stated principles, they are more likely to act with integrity, even in challenging circumstances. However, when there is a disconnect between what a company professes and the reality of its culture, individuals may feel pressured to compromise their ethics, leading to actions that can harm both the organization and its stakeholders.

Building a Strong Ethical Culture
To foster an environment where ethical behavior is the norm, companies must ensure that their corporate values are not merely words on a page but are actively embodied and reinforced throughout their culture. This involves promoting transparency, fairness, and responsibility in all business dealings and creating a space where employees at all levels are empowered to speak up and act in alignment with these values.

Leaders play a crucial role in this process by exemplifying ethical behavior and establishing a culture where ethical dilemmas are openly discussed and addressed without fear of retribution. Regular training on ethical decision-making and clear communication about the company's values and expectations help to underscore the significance of ethics in the workplace.

Moreover, recognizing and rewarding ethical behavior shows that integrity is valued as highly as financial achievements. By doing so, companies can cultivate a strong ethical culture that enhances employee well-being and contributes to long-term business success.

Ethics in business extends beyond individual and organizational boundaries to include international organizations and countries. It is essential that these entities uphold ethical standards and values consistently. If these values are not applied fairly across all levels, these bodies risk losing credibility.

By aligning personal, corporate, and global ethical values, organizations foster a workplace where employees feel that their values are respected and supported, encouraging them to act with integrity even in challenging situations. Promoting a robust ethical framework allows companies to build trust, mitigate legal and reputational risks, and create an environment where ethical conduct is a cornerstone of professional behavior.

Summary

In this chapter, we have explored the profound impact of organizational culture on a company's success, employee engagement, and overall identity. Culture is not just a set of values written on paper; it is a living, dynamic force that influences every aspect of an organization. However, maintaining a healthy and positive culture requires ongoing effort and, most importantly, active involvement from both leadership and employees at all levels.

When issues arise within the corporate culture—such as a misalignment between espoused and enacted values or the emergence of toxic behaviors—the role of managers and leaders becomes critical. If these problems are not addressed promptly and effectively, they can escalate, leading to a decline in employee morale, a breakdown in collaboration, and ultimately, diminished organizational performance.

Leaders must remain vigilant in identifying cultural issues and commit to resolving them before they escalate. This involves leading by example and fostering an environment where employees feel safe to voice concerns, and where feedback is actively encouraged and addressed.

At the same time, the responsibility for sustaining a positive organizational culture does not rest solely with leadership; it is a shared responsibility that extends to every employee. Every individual, regardless of their position, contributes to the culture through their actions, decisions, and interactions. When employees at all levels embody the company's values, they reinforce a culture of integrity, collaboration, and innovation.

In summary, a thriving organizational culture is nurtured by leadership and sustained through collective employee efforts. Everyone is responsible for upholding company values and addressing threats to them. By working together, leaders and employees can secure the organization's future and foster a workplace where all can thrive and contribute meaningfully.

Chapter Four

Conducting Effective Meetings

M eetings are a fundamental aspect of professional life, yet they are often met with frustration rather than enthusiasm. How many times have you heard someone compliment a meeting with phrases like, "we had a very productive meeting"? Unfortunately, such positive sentiments are rare. In fact, meetings are frequently viewed as time-consuming, unproductive, and sometimes, unnecessary.

These complaints highlight a fundamental issue: many meetings are poorly planned, lack clear objectives, or involve participants who do not need to be there. However, when conducted effectively, meetings can be powerful tools for decision-making, collaboration, and driving organizational progress.

Despite the common complaints, meetings are crucial for the smooth operation of any organization. They serve as a platform for collaboration, decision-making, and communication. However, the key to effective meetings lies in understanding their purpose and conducting them in a way that maximizes productivity.

Before scheduling any meeting, it is crucial to clearly define its purpose and the desired outcomes.

Types of Meetings

Meetings come in various forms, each designed to serve specific purposes and audiences. Understanding the different types of meetings is crucial for effective planning, execution, and achieving desired outcomes. Below are common types of meetings:

One-on-One Meetings

Typically held on a regular or as-needed basis, one-on-one meetings provide a unique opportunity for personalized discussions between two individuals, often a manager and an employee. These meetings are essential for addressing personal development, performance feedback, and discussing sensitive matters in a private setting.

Not all one-on-one meetings need to take place in formal environments. In some cases, informal settings, such as lunch meetings or casual chats in the cafeteria, can foster a more relaxed atmosphere, making it easier for both parties to engage in open and honest dialogue. These informal interactions can help build rapport and encourage honest communication that may be limited in a more formal setting.

For example, if a sales manager notices that a team member has been underperforming, they may choose to address the issue in a relaxed, informal setting like lunch. The employee may feel more at ease sharing concerns, and the manager can offer constructive feedback in a non-confrontational manner. Together, they can develop an action plan with clear goals and support, such as additional training. This highlights the value of informal one-on-one meetings in fostering open communication and stronger working relationships.

Staff Meetings

Usually held weekly, biweekly, or monthly, staff meetings bring the entire team together to focus on updates, planning, and coordination. These meetings are critical for ensuring that team members are aligned with ongoing projects and company objectives.

In a technology startup, weekly meetings are a common practice to ensure that all team members are aligned with the current goals and tasks. Each member provides a brief update on their activities from the previous week, outlines their plans for the current week, and discusses any obstacles they are encountering. These meetings are typically short, around 30 – 60 minutes, but they are crucial for keeping the team on track, identifying potential issues early, and providing resources as needed.

Pre-Shift and Brief Meetings

Pre-shift and briefing meetings are short, focused discussions held before the start of a shift or project. They aim to set clear objectives, review key tasks, and ensure all team members are aligned and fully prepared for the work ahead. These meetings play a vital role in fostering communication, clarifying roles, and identifying any immediate challenges or priorities that require attention.

For example, in a manufacturing plant, a pre-shift meeting might involve supervisors reviewing the day's production targets,

91

assigning specific responsibilities, and addressing any safety concerns or operational updates. This ensures that the team begins the shift with a clear understanding of their goals and expectations, promoting efficiency and reducing potential issues during the workday.

In environments like retail or hospitality, pre-shift meetings (Figure 11) might focus on customer service goals, special promotions, or team responsibilities for the day, ensuring that everyone is on the same page. Additionally, toolbox talks are often incorporated into these meetings in industries like construction or manufacturing, where safety is a primary concern. These talks address specific safety topics to ensure that all team members are aware of and can mitigate risks associated with their tasks.

By holding these quick but effective meetings, organizations can improve coordination, enhance performance, and ensure a smoother workflow throughout the shift.

Figure 11. Pre-Shift Meeting

Brainstorming and Problem-Solving Meetings

Brainstorming meetings are designed to generate creative ideas and solutions to specific problems. In these sessions, participants are encouraged to think freely and offer innovative solutions without fear of criticism. Problem-solving meetings focus on identifying challenges and working collaboratively to develop actionable solutions.

For example, a company facing declining sales might hold a brainstorming session with its marketing team to generate fresh campaign ideas. These types of meetings are crucial for fostering innovation and driving business growth.

Group Meetings

Held quarterly or semi-annually, group meetings involve larger teams or departments and typically focus on broader topics such as departmental goals or cross-functional projects. These meetings are ideal for discussing strategic initiatives that require input from multiple departments.

For instance, a company may hold quarterly meetings between its marketing and sales teams to align on strategies, review sales data, and plan joint campaigns. These meetings foster collaboration and ensure that key departments work toward shared objectives.

Corporate Meetings

Often held annually or as needed, corporate meetings involve the entire organization and address significant issues such as mergers, acquisitions, or policy changes. These meetings are typically used

93

to communicate major decisions and provide updates on the company's direction.

For example, at an annual corporate meeting, a CEO may present the company's performance over the past year and outline strategic goals for the year ahead. This type of meeting fosters transparency and direct communication between leadership and employees, building trust and engagement across the organization.

Skip-level Meetings

Skip-level meetings are a vital tool where senior managers meet directly with employees who report to supervisors beneath them, bypassing middle management. These meetings offer senior leaders valuable firsthand insights into operational challenges and employee experiences. By enabling direct communication, skip-level meetings help build trust, promote transparency, and ensure that senior leaders remain connected to the organization's day-to-day realities. Unfortunately, many organizations do not implement this effective practice.

Many employees express concerns about a disconnect between themselves and upper management, often feeling that senior leaders are out of touch with their challenges and more focused on pleasing their own superiors. This perceived gap can create a sense of hierarchy that alienates lower-level employees. Skip-level meetings address these concerns by offering employees a platform to voice their experiences, ideas, and concerns directly to senior management.

This practice bridges the communication gap and helps dismantle the sense of hierarchy, making senior leaders more approachable and engaged with the team's needs. By implementing skip-level meetings, organizations can cultivate a more inclusive and transparent culture where every employee feels valued and heard.

For example, in a prominent manufacturing firm, the Vice President of Operations initiated quarterly skip-level meetings with production line employees. During these sessions, the VP asked open-ended questions about the work environment, safety procedures, and suggestions for operational improvements. With their direct supervisors not present, employees felt more comfortable sharing candid feedback. As a result, the VP gained valuable insights from the ground level, leading to actionable improvements in safety practices and operational efficiency. This demonstrates the tangible benefits of skip-level meetings in promoting a more open, transparent, and effective workplace culture.

Various types of meetings serve distinct purposes within an organization, from fostering innovation in brainstorming sessions to building trust in one-on-one meetings. Pre-shift and brief meetings promote continuous improvement, while skip-level and corporate meetings foster communication across different levels of the organization. Understanding and effectively utilizing each meeting type ensures better alignment, collaboration, and success in achieving organizational goals.

Effective Meetings

Not every issue requires a meeting. Understanding when to hold a meeting is crucial to avoid wasting time and resources.

Meetings should be held in situations such as:

- Seeking information or advice from your team.
- Involving your group in solving a problem or making a decision.
- Clarifying an issue that needs further explanation.
- Sharing concerns with your group.

Meeting Agenda

Effective meetings require thorough preparation. A well-prepared meeting is more likely to achieve its objectives and be seen as valuable by the participants.

A well-crafted agenda is fundamental to the success of any meeting. It should include:

Approval of Previous Meeting Minutes: Confirm the minutes from the previous meeting, assuming they were not approved earlier through offline channels. This is necessary if formal approval is required.

Follow-Up on Action Items: Review the progress of action items from prior meetings to ensure accountability and continuous progress.

Main Agenda Items: List the key topics for discussion, clearly indicating the owner of each item and the time allocated for each to ensure focused and efficient discussions.

Open Floor: Allow time for additional topics not listed on the initial agenda, giving participants the opportunity to bring up new issues or concerns.

Logistics for Next Meeting: Confirm the time, date, and location of the next meeting, and invite suggestions for agenda items to ensure ongoing engagement and preparedness.

Meeting Minutes

Accurate and consistent meeting minutes are essential for keeping track of decisions made, actions to be taken, and follow-up items (Figure 12). It is important to assign someone to take the minutes, usually the meeting facilitator, an administrative assistant, or a designated team member.

Consistent minute-taking helps maintain the continuity of the meeting process. Changing the minute-taker frequently can lead to inconsistencies, loss of information, and difficulty in tracking actions from previous meetings.

One of the main pitfalls of unprofessional meetings is losing track of previous actions, which leads to a lack of follow-through and repeated discussions on the same topics. This wastes time and undermines the significance of the issues being discussed.

Meeting Minutes

Date: [Meeting's date].

Time: [Start time] - [End time].

Location: [Meeting's location].

Attendees:
[List of attendees].

Absentees:
[List of absentees].

Agenda:
- Approval of previous meeting minutes.
- Agenda items - [List each agenda item and the presenter's name].
- Open discussion - Any topics not covered under the main agenda items.

Minutes:
- Approval of previous meeting minutes: The minutes from the previous meeting on [insert date] were approved unanimously.
- Agenda items: [Provide a brief summary of the discussion, decisions, or unresolved issues for each item].
- Open discussion: [Summary of discussions].

Bin List (Future Items):
- [List items to be discussed in future meetings].

Action Items:
- [Review the previous action items assigned to the owners and monitor the deadlines closely. Maintain this list in a separate document to consolidate all items in one place, ensuring easy access and efficient follow-up.].

Next Meeting:
- Date: [Next meeting date].
- Time: [Next meeting time].
- Location: [Next meeting location].

Meeting Adjourned:
- Time: [Time meeting was adjourned].
- Minutes prepared by: [Your name].

Figure 12. Example of a Meeting Minutes Template

In a construction company, project meetings are critical for coordinating between different teams, including architects, engineers, and contractors. During a large infrastructure project, the project manager insisted on detailed meeting minutes to ensure that every decision, action item, and responsibility was clearly documented.

This practice proved vital when, months later, a dispute arose about the specifications of a particular component. The meeting minutes provided clear evidence of the agreed-upon details, which helped resolve the dispute quickly and kept the project on track.

Right Participants

The success of a meeting often depends on having the right people in attendance. Invite only those individuals who can contribute meaningfully to the discussion and help achieve the meeting's objectives.

For instance, if the meeting is focused on an emergency plan or a major strategic change, it may be necessary to invite a broader group to ensure everyone is informed and has the opportunity to ask questions.

Additionally, consider whether all attendees need to be present for the entire meeting or only for specific parts. This approach helps to respect everyone's time and keeps the meeting focused.

At a startup, the CEO noticed that meetings were becoming too large and unmanageable, often involving people who did not need to be there. To address this, the CEO implemented a "lean meeting" policy, where only those directly involved in the agenda items were invited. For example, a product development meeting included only the product manager, lead engineer, and marketing lead, rather than the entire development team. This change made the meetings more focused and efficient, allowing participants to dive deeper into the issues without distractions. Meeting minutes can be shared with others as needed to keep everyone informed instead.

Conducting the Meeting

The effectiveness of a meeting relies on both thorough preparation and its execution. To maximize productivity and efficiency, consider the following best practices:

Timing: Schedule the meeting when it suits the majority of attendees.

Reminders: Send reminders in advance and strive to avoid rescheduling unless absolutely necessary.

Preparation: Distribute the meeting agenda in advance to ensure participants are well-prepared and arrive early to organize the space and verify that all necessary arrangements are in place.

Roles: Designate someone to take minutes and assign a timekeeper to ensure discussions stay within allotted times.

Role of the Meeting Facilitator

The facilitator plays an indispensable role in steering the meeting. It is crucial for the facilitator to remain neutral, avoiding any biases or predetermined conclusions. The facilitator should encourage contributions from all participants, promote active engagement, and attentively listen to diverse viewpoints.

To keep discussions on point, the facilitator needs to manage any off-topic conversations and prevent the meeting from straying from its agenda. If a topic requires more time than scheduled, it may be appropriate to arrange a follow-up meeting with relevant parties to continue the dialogue. This approach ensures that meetings are productive and conducive to achieving their objectives.

Handling Difficult Personalities

Meetings often gather individuals with diverse personalities, which can sometimes lead to conflicts or unproductive interactions. Here are some effective strategies for managing challenging personalities in meetings:

Setting Ground Rules: Begin the meeting by establishing clear behavioral ground rules. These should include respecting others' opinions and avoiding interruptions to promote a constructive dialogue.

Addressing Dominant Participants: At times, a single participant may dominate a group discussion, limiting others' opportunities to contribute. A tactful way to address this is by redirecting the conversation with a respectful prompt—for instance, by saying, "I appreciate your insights; let us also hear from someone who has not spoken yet."

However, if this approach does not lead to more balanced participation, further strategies may be necessary. One effective method is to reinforce ground rules by reminding everyone of the importance of equal speaking time, which helps frame inclusivity as a shared value rather than a personal criticism. Introducing structured turn-taking can also help, such as inviting participants to speak in order, setting brief time limits, or directing questions to quieter members. If the issue persists and begins to affect group dynamics, it may be appropriate to address the matter privately with the individual—expressing appreciation for their enthusiasm while encouraging them to help create space for others.

In more formal settings, facilitators may also rely on tools such as "parking lots" to manage off-topic remarks, use breakout groups to diversify participation, or apply visual cues and time moderation in virtual environments. Ultimately, managing dominant voices requires both sensitivity and structure to ensure that all participants feel heard and valued.

Managing Conflict: Should conflicts arise, address them with calm professionalism. Acknowledge differing viewpoints and maintain a focus on the meeting's objectives to ensure discussions remain productive.

At a company's product development meeting, the team gathered to shape the design of an eagerly anticipated new release. Midway through the session, a spirited debate between two members escalated into a tense standoff over the design direction. Recognizing the rising tension, the meeting facilitator stepped in, acknowledging the value in both perspectives and suggesting a short break to allow emotions to cool. When the team reconvened, the facilitator refocused the discussion on the ultimate goal — creating a standout product. With renewed energy and clarity, the group reached a compromise that combined the strongest aspects of each proposal, leading to an improved design that ultimately achieved remarkable success in the market.

Post-Meeting Follow-Up

The conclusion of a meeting does not signify the end of the work; effective follow-up is essential to ensure that decisions made, and actions agreed upon are implemented. Here is an effective approach to managing post-meeting activities:

Distribute Meeting Minutes: Promptly share the meeting minutes with all attendees and any other relevant stakeholders who need to stay informed. This record serves as a reference for the discussions held, decisions made, and individual responsibilities assigned, helping to keep everyone aligned and accountable. Approval of the minutes can be obtained offline or at the beginning of the next meeting.

Action Item Tracking: Establish a robust system for tracking action items to ensure progress is monitored effectively and efficiency is maintained (Figure 13). Utilize tools such as shared documents, project management software, or structured update mechanisms to streamline this process. Clearly defined deadlines and assigned responsibilities are essential for promoting accountability and driving task completion.

Actions Required Tracking List					
Date Assigned	Assigned to	Description	Due Date	Status	Remarks

Figure 13. Sample of Actions Required Tracking List

To maintain clarity and continuity, closed items should be archived systematically for future reference, while open items must remain

103

actively tracked and regularly reviewed. Consistent follow-up is critical to prevent the common inefficiencies associated with meeting outcomes.

Feedback Loop: Solicit feedback from participants regarding the meeting's effectiveness. Encourage comments on what aspects were successful and what areas need improvement. This feedback is invaluable for enhancing the quality and efficiency of future meetings.

For example, after a strategic planning session at a mid-sized manufacturing firm, the CEO promptly sent a detailed follow-up email to all department heads summarizing the key decisions and assigned tasks. To ensure the strategic objectives are actively pursued and not merely theoretical, the CEO also scheduled a follow-up meeting one month later to assess progress. This systematic approach ensures that strategic initiatives move forward as planned.

By implementing these strategies, you can navigate complex personality dynamics effectively, ensuring that your meetings are both productive and inclusive.

Virtual Meetings

With the rise of remote work, virtual meetings have become more common. Conducting effective virtual meetings requires some additional considerations:

Technology Preparation: Ensure that all participants have access to the necessary technology and know how to use it. This includes video conferencing tools, screen-sharing capabilities, and collaborative platforms.

Engagement Strategies: Virtual meetings can be challenging in terms of maintaining engagement. Use tools like polls, and visual aids to keep participants involved.

Time Zone Considerations: When scheduling meetings with participants in different time zones, be mindful of the timing to ensure it is convenient for everyone.

A global company needed to hold a virtual meeting with teams from three different continents. The meeting organizer carefully scheduled the meeting at a time that was reasonable for all participants, considering the various time zones. The meeting included interactive elements such as real-time polls and a collaborative whiteboard tool that allowed everyone to contribute ideas visually. By the end of the meeting, despite the geographical distance, the team felt connected and aligned on the project goals.

Whenever feasible, prioritize scheduling face-to-face meetings, as they are generally more productive. However, for multi-site organizations or participants unable to attend in person due to valid reasons, online meetings can be arranged.

Effective Delegation in Meetings

Effective delegation is crucial when a team member is unable to attend a meeting. In such cases, the absent employee should delegate a representative who is well-informed and capable of contributing meaningfully to the discussion.

This delegate should possess background knowledge on the topics to be discussed, be up-to-date on any required actions, and be able to provide valuable input during the meeting. Simply sending any person to fill a seat is insufficient; the delegate must be prepared to engage fully and represent the absent member's interests and responsibilities.

Delegating effectively ensures that the meeting's momentum is maintained, decisions are made with all necessary information, and there is continuity in addressing ongoing issues. It also demonstrates respect for the meeting process and the time of all participants, ensuring that the meeting remains productive and focused on achieving its objectives.

In a software development company, the product manager was unable to attend a critical meeting about an upcoming product launch due to a scheduling conflict. Instead of sending a random team member, the product manager delegated the lead developer, who was deeply involved in the project and understood both the technical and strategic aspects of the product.

Before the meeting, the product manager briefed the lead developer on the key points to address, including updates on the project timeline and specific decisions that needed to be made. During the meeting, the lead developer was able to provide valuable insights, answer questions, and ensure that the product manager's priorities were represented. As a result, the meeting was productive, and the team made significant progress towards the launch without any setbacks caused by the manager's absence.

This example illustrates the importance of choosing the right delegate—someone who is prepared, knowledgeable, and capable of contributing to the meeting's success. By delegating effectively, the product manager ensured that the project stayed on track and that the meeting remained a valuable use of everyone's time.

Continuous Improvement of Meeting Practices

Organizations should continually assess and enhance their meeting practices to ensure they remain productive and effective. This ongoing improvement can be achieved through several strategies:

Regular Reviews: Conduct periodic evaluations of meeting effectiveness by soliciting feedback from attendees. Use this feedback to identify areas for improvement, such as adjusting the frequency of meetings or modifying their structure to better meet team needs.

Training and Development: Invest in training programs for employees, particularly those in leadership positions, on conducting effective meetings. This training could cover topics like facilitation skills, time management, and conflict resolution to equip leaders with the tools they need to lead productive discussions.

Experimentation: Be open to experimenting with various meeting formats and technologies. For instance, consider implementing shorter, more frequent check-ins as an alternative to lengthy meetings, or adopt new technological tools to enhance collaborative efforts.

For example, a financial services firm recognized that their weekly meetings were becoming progressively unproductive, characterized by frequent overruns and diminishing participant engagement. In response, the leadership initiated a continuous improvement program specifically for meeting practices. They implemented a feedback system to gather insights directly from meeting participants, provided targeted training on facilitation techniques for managers, and tested different meeting formats. These changes led to a marked improvement in meeting efficiency and participant engagement within just a few months.

By regularly reviewing and refining meeting practices, organizations can significantly enhance the productivity of their meetings and ensure they effectively contribute to business objectives.

Creating a Meeting Culture

The effectiveness of meetings is heavily influenced by an organization's culture. Developing a productive meeting culture involves several key practices, such as:

Valuing Everyone's Time: Fostering a culture that views meetings as a productive tool for coordination and decision-making reflects an organization's commitment to respecting employees' time. This includes starting and ending meetings on time, adhering to a clear agenda, and holding meetings only when necessary.

If an individual is consistently late and shows a lack of seriousness in attending meetings, the issue should be addressed privately and professionally. It's important to clarify that this behavior not only affects the team's effectiveness but also reflects negatively on the individual's performance—particularly in areas such as discipline, commitment, and active participation.

If the behavior continues, further corrective steps may be necessary, such as involving the direct supervisor or assigning the individual a key opening role in the meeting to encourage timely attendance. In some cases, persistent lateness may indicate disengagement or a decline in accountability, which should be discussed within the context of overall job performance.

Encouraging Open Communication: Foster an environment that allows all participants to feel comfortable expressing their thoughts and ideas. This inclusion of diverse perspectives enhances decision-making and overall meeting productivity.

Recognition and Appreciation: Regularly acknowledge and appreciate contributions made during meetings. Simple gestures, such as thanking participants for their input or recognizing the successful completion of tasks from previous meetings, can boost morale and engagement.

Embracing Differing Opinions: Diverse opinions should not be viewed negatively; rather, they are natural and essential. It is crucial to engage in discussions about these differences substantively and without taking them personally. It is essential to ensure that disagreements among participants do not carry over into personal conflicts beyond the meetings, as this can undermine team spirit.

By adopting similar strategies, organizations can create a meeting culture that respects participants' time and promotes a supportive, productive space for sharing ideas and making decisions.

Summary

Conducting effective meetings is not merely a logistical task; it is a crucial element for enhancing productivity and driving the success of any organization. While some may think that running an effective meeting is straightforward or intuitive, the reality is more complex.

Despite their experience, many senior managers have struggled to conduct truly effective meetings. The skill requires careful observation, continuous learning, and improvement over time. Simply reading about best practices and applying them in real-world settings can significantly enhance one's ability to lead impactful meetings.

Meetings that are well-planned and executed can transcend routine gatherings, becoming vital instruments for robust communication, strategic decision-making, and effective problem-solving.

This chapter has provided a detailed framework designed to guide leaders in organizing meetings that are efficient, engaging, and rich in outcomes. By clearly understanding the objectives of each meeting, meticulously preparing for them, thoughtfully selecting the right participants, and managing the proceedings with professionalism, leaders can ensure that meetings serve as valuable assets rather than obligatory engagements.

Adopting the principles discussed here can transform the perception and conduct of meetings within an organization. When these principles are applied, meetings can become vital opportunities for fostering collaboration, sparking innovation, and facilitating organizational growth. This shift can dramatically enhance the productivity of individual team members and, consequently, the organization as a whole.

Moreover, incorporating social elements and off-site activities, such as team-building exercises, adds another layer of value. These interactions enhance interpersonal relationships among team members, strengthening the cohesion and morale of the team. Such activities are not just enjoyable; they also break the monotony of routine work, boosting productivity and commitment to the company's goals.

In summary, by extending beyond traditional meeting management to embrace a holistic approach—including social bonding and professional development—organizations can foster a more engaging and supportive work environment. This comprehensive approach ensures that meetings are no longer viewed as mere checkboxes on the corporate agenda but as pivotal, strategic tools that significantly contribute to the company's broader success.

Chapter Five

Effective Negotiation

Negotiation is an essential skill that influences both our personal and professional lives. It is a dynamic process in which two or more parties engage to reach an agreement that is not only acceptable but ideally beneficial for all involved. Whether it is negotiating the terms of a business contract, a salary, or even deciding on vacation plans with family, the principles of effective negotiation remain constant. At its core, negotiation is about communication, understanding, and strategy. The ability to negotiate effectively can transform conflicts into opportunities for collaboration and mutual gain.

The art of negotiation involves securing the best possible deal while also building and maintaining relationships. Effective negotiators are those who understand that long-term success often depends on the ability to forge partnerships where all parties feel valued.

Interests vs. Positions

A key concept in negotiation is distinguishing between positions and interests. A position represents what a party explicitly demands, such as a high starting price in a sales negotiation. In contrast, interests are the deeper motivations or needs driving those demands—such as the desire for financial stability, securing a long-term business relationship, or gaining market share.

Recognizing this distinction allows negotiators to move beyond surface-level demands and understand what truly matters to the other party. For instance, in a workplace negotiation, an employee might request a higher salary (position), but their underlying interests could include career growth, job satisfaction, or recognition for their efforts. By identifying these interests, the employer can offer alternatives, such as professional development opportunities or a performance-based bonus, addressing both the employee's needs and the company's budgetary constraints.

This approach paves the way for creative, win-win solutions that meet the interests of all parties. Instead of getting locked into rigid positions, negotiators can explore multiple paths to satisfy the underlying interests, ultimately leading to more sustainable and mutually beneficial agreements.

Different Negotiation Styles

Negotiation is deeply rooted in understanding the dynamics of human interactions as well as the substantive issues being discussed. Over time, various negotiation styles have emerged, tailored to different situations and personality types. Recognizing these styles, both in oneself and in others, is essential for effectively navigating the complex landscape of negotiations. This concept aligns with what is known as Lewicki and Hiam's Negotiation Matrix (Figure 14), which categorizes negotiation strategies to optimize outcomes based on the interaction of these styles.

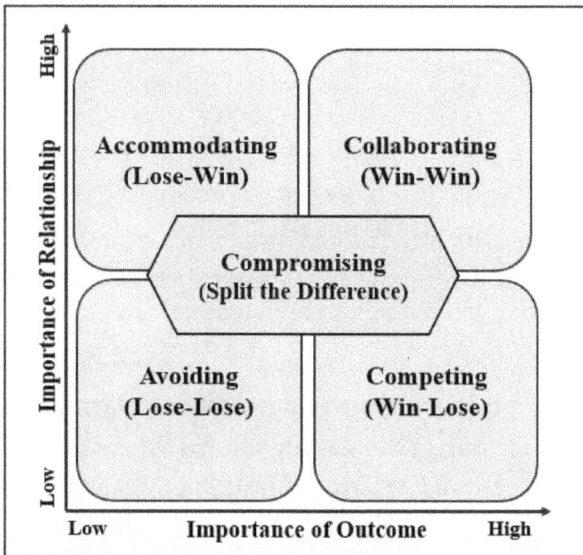

Figure 14. Lewicki and Hiam's Negotiation Matrix

Competing Style: Focuses on winning, sometimes at the expense of the other party. This approach is effective when the stakes are high, and the negotiator holds a strong position. However, it can strain relationships which could be detrimental in long-term dealings.

Collaborating Style: Seeks to find a win-win solution by addressing the interests of all parties. This approach fosters cooperation and is ideal in scenarios where long-term relationships are valued. Collaborative negotiators focus on open communication, transparency, and mutual respect.

Avoiding Style: Avoids engaging fully in discussions, often used to sidestep potential conflicts. This approach proves most effective in scenarios where the risks are minimal, and the issues are not critical.

However, over-reliance on this style can lead to significant concerns being neglected or unresolved.

Accommodating Style: Prioritizes the needs of the other party over one's own. This can be effective when preserving the relationship is more important than the outcome of the negotiation. However, overuse of this style might lead to resentment or feelings of being undervalued.

Compromising Style: Involves both parties making concessions to reach a middle ground. This can be useful when time is limited or when both parties have relatively equal power. However, it may result in a solution that is acceptable but not optimal for either party.

Successful negotiators are often those who can adapt their style to the situation and the needs of the parties involved. Understanding when to compete, collaborate, compromise, avoid, or accommodate can make the difference between a deal that merely satisfies and one that truly benefits all involved.

The Principles of Negotiation

Negotiation is founded on several core principles that, when properly understood and implemented, can significantly enhance the likelihood of achieving a successful agreement. Key among these principles are effective communication, empathy, and flexibility.

Communication: Effective communication is key to conveying your position clearly and understanding the other party's perspective. This includes active listening, asking open-ended questions, and avoiding misunderstandings through clarification.

Empathy: Understanding the emotions and motivations of the other party can create a more cooperative atmosphere. Empathy allows negotiators to see the situation from multiple angles, which can lead to creative problem-solving.

Flexibility: While having clear goals is important, so is the ability to adapt to new information and changing circumstances. Flexibility in negotiation means being open to alternative solutions that may not have been considered initially but could lead to a better overall outcome.

One of the most notable examples of high-stakes negotiation in the business world was the merger of two major technology companies. The negotiation was complex, covering the financial terms, integration of company cultures, protection of intellectual property, and retention of key employees. The negotiators from both companies spent months preparing, understanding the market landscape, and aligning on strategic goals.

During the negotiation, the principle of empathy played a significant role. The acquiring company understood the concerns of the smaller company, particularly around job security for its employees. As a result, they proposed a plan that included retention bonuses and career development programs for the acquired company's employees. This move facilitated the merger and helped retain valuable talent post-acquisition.

In the end, the merger was successful, with both companies achieving their goals. The larger company expanded its product portfolio, while the smaller company gained access to new markets and resources. This case study highlights how a well-prepared and empathetic approach to negotiation can lead to a win-win outcome.

A common misconception in negotiation is the fixed-pie perception—the belief that one party's gain is automatically the other party's loss. This view often leads to a zero-sum approach, where negotiators focus on dividing a limited set of resources rather than exploring opportunities for mutual gain. This mindset can cause negotiators to adopt one of three strategies: conceding to the other side (soft approach), preparing for an attack (hard approach), or compromising, which may prevent both parties from achieving their best possible outcomes.

To illustrate the dangers of the fixed-pie perception, consider the story of two siblings fighting over an orange. Both wanted the whole orange and decided to split it in half. Later, they discovered that one sibling only needed the juice, while the other needed the peel for baking. Had they communicated their true interests, both could have achieved 100% of what they wanted. This example demonstrates the importance of understanding underlying interests to find win-win solutions.

Preparation

Preparation is often highlighted as the most critical factor in achieving success in negotiations. Many experts believe that up to 80% of a negotiation's effectiveness is determined before the parties even meet at the bargaining table. Effective preparation can decisively influence the outcome by ensuring that all relevant information about the situation and the parties involved is thoroughly gathered.

This process involves three essential steps: self-assessment in negotiation, assessment of the other party, and assessment of the situation. Each of these steps, which will be detailed subsequently, forms the foundation for developing a strategic approach aimed at achieving the desired outcomes in any negotiation scenario.

A compelling example of effective negotiation preparation is illustrated by the experience of Layaan, a small business owner who was negotiating a lease for a new retail space. Confronted with an initial rental rate significantly above her budget, Layaan chose not to give up or walk away from the negotiation. Instead, she engaged in meticulous preparation, researching comparable properties in the area, analyzing current market trends, and crafting a persuasive presentation of the benefits her business would bring to the landlord, such as consistent occupancy and increased customer traffic.

Her comprehensive and well-prepared strategy led to a successful negotiation, resulting in a rental agreement that met her budgetary constraints and included a six-month rent reduction. This case underscores how thorough preparation, strategic communication, and a commitment to finding mutually beneficial solutions are crucial for successful negotiations.

Step 1: Self-Assessment

Self-assessment is a critical component of negotiation preparation. It involves evaluating your goals, identifying your Best Alternative to a Negotiated Agreement (BATNA), and understanding your emotional triggers. Knowing what you truly want, what you are willing to compromise on, and what your alternatives are if the negotiation fails, are all essential for effective negotiation.

119

Avoiding common pitfalls in self-assessment is a crucial step in preparation for negotiations, it is common for individuals to set targets that are either unattainably high or undesirably low. Goals that are too ambitious can lead to deadlocks in negotiations, as they may be beyond what is realistically achievable, while setting them too low can result in accepting outcomes that are less than what could have been achieved. Another frequent error is overconfidence, where negotiators overestimate their skills or the probability of securing a favorable deal.

To illustrate, consider a sales manager negotiating a contract. If she sets an unrealistically high sales target, it might lead to deadlock with the client who may find the terms unacceptable. Conversely, setting a very low target might lead to a quick agreement but could result in leaving money on the table by not maximizing potential earnings. Regular reassessment of one's position and maintaining grounded expectations are vital for avoiding such pitfalls, ensuring that negotiations are both realistic and effective.

Understanding Your BATNA

BATNA, or Best Alternative to a Negotiated Agreement, is a critical concept in negotiations as it represents the most advantageous alternative action a negotiator can take if the current negotiation fails to produce an agreement. Possessing a strong BATNA grants significant leverage, enabling the negotiator to confidently walk away from any deal that does not meet their minimum requirements.

Consider the example of Alex, an MBA student who receives a job offer from Company X with a salary of $6,000 per month, along with additional allowances and benefits. However, Alex's preferred employer is Company Y. In this case, the offer from Company X represents Alex's BATNA. If Company Y offers a lower salary or fewer benefits, Alex can use his BATNA as leverage to negotiate better terms or opt for the more favorable offer from Company X. Effectively utilizing a BATNA sets a benchmark below which a deal should not be accepted, ensuring the negotiator's position remains strategic and well-informed.

Reservation Point
The reservation point in negotiation is a quantifiable value or condition that represents your absolute limit—beyond which you are unwilling to proceed with the negotiation.

To clarify the distinction and avoid confusion, note that BATNA (Best Alternative to a Negotiated Agreement) focuses on alternatives outside the current negotiation, offering a fallback plan if no agreement is reached. In contrast, the reservation point specifically pertains to the least acceptable agreement within the negotiation itself. While the BATNA represents the best alternative if negotiations fail, the reservation point defines the minimum acceptable outcome within the negotiation.

For example, if you are selling a car, your reservation point might be $5,000—the lowest price you would accept. However, your BATNA could be to keep the car, as it remains reliable and meets your needs, providing a different kind of value than selling it at an undesirably low price.

The Zone of Possible Agreement (ZOPA)
ZOPA exists where the reservation points of the negotiating parties overlap, indicating a range within which an agreement is achievable. By understanding both the reservation point and the BATNA,

negotiators are better equipped to effectively navigate discussions, setting clear boundaries and identifying viable areas for agreement.

Consider a scenario as depicted in Figure 15, involving a buyer and a seller. The seller's reservation point is $6,000, which is the minimum price they are prepared to accept, informed by their BATNA and alternatives. Conversely, the buyer's reservation point is $7,500, which is the maximum they are willing to pay. The range that overlaps—between $6,000 and $7,500—constitutes the ZOPA, where an agreement is feasible, and both parties can potentially find common ground on price.

Understanding these dynamics is crucial for negotiators to achieve a mutually satisfactory agreement.

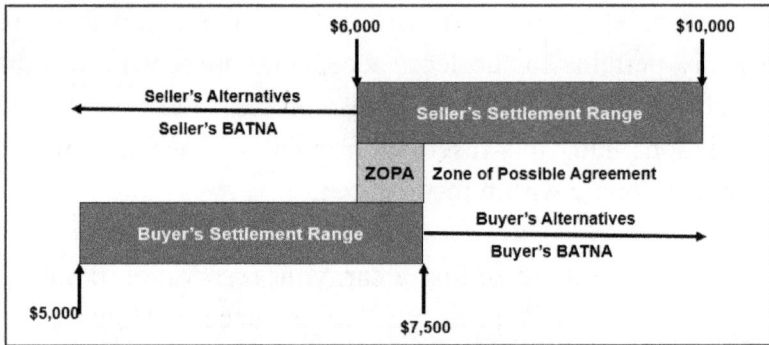

Figure 15. BATNA and ZOPA

It is also crucial to recognize that a ZOPA may not always be present in negotiations. This occurs when there is no overlap between the acceptable terms of both parties. For instance, if the seller's lowest acceptable price is higher than the maximum price a buyer is prepared to pay, then a ZOPA does not exist, making an agreement impossible under the current negotiation terms.

As shown in Figure 16, the seller's reservation point is $8,000, the lowest price they are willing to accept, while the buyer's reservation point is $7,000, the highest they are prepared to pay. The absence of overlap indicates that no ZOPA exists in this negotiation scenario. This lack of a ZOPA underscores that reaching an agreement is not feasible without significant adjustments to the terms or expectations by one or both parties, highlighting the necessity for openness to alternative solutions or flexibility in negotiation terms.

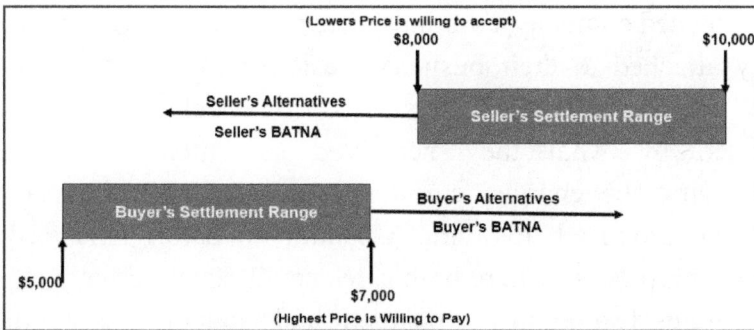

Figure 16. BATNA and No ZOPA

Emotional Control in Negotiation

Negotiations can often be emotionally intense, particularly when the stakes involved are significant. Emotions like anger, frustration, or anxiety can impair judgment, potentially leading to decisions that may not align with your best interests. Effective negotiation includes recognizing and managing your emotional responses.

One method to maintain emotional control is to pause and take a break when feelings become overwhelming. A brief respite from the

123

negotiation table can help in regaining composure and perspective. Additionally, engaging in mindfulness and practicing deep-breathing exercises before and during negotiations can aid in maintaining calm and focus.

Empathy also plays a crucial role in emotional control. Understanding the perspective of the opposing party enables a more effective response to their concerns and objections. This approach fosters a constructive atmosphere and promotes more productive discussions.

For instance, in a tense business negotiation over the sale of a family-owned company, emotions were notably intense. The sellers, deeply attached to their business, hesitated to accept terms they believed undervalued their life's work. Conversely, the buyers were frustrated by what they perceived as unrealistic demands. Recognizing the charged emotional landscape, the buyers' lead negotiator proposed involving a neutral mediator. This mediator facilitated a process where both sides could constructively express their feelings, leading to an empathetic and collaborative negotiation environment.

The outcome was an agreement that respected the sellers' legacy and provided a fair arrangement for the buyers, illustrating the critical importance of managing emotions in negotiations, especially where personal and financial interests are deeply intertwined.

Managing High-Pressure Negotiations
High-pressure negotiations, involving tight deadlines or substantial financial implications, require thorough preparation and psychological resilience. In these scenarios, maintaining

composure, thinking strategically, and making informed decisions under pressure are essential skills.

To navigate high-pressure negotiations effectively, consider these strategies:

- **Break Down the Process:** Segment the negotiation into distinct phases. Tackling one issue at a time helps mitigate the stress associated with the complexity of the deal, making the overall process more manageable.

- **Stay Focused on Your Goals:** Maintain a clear vision of your long-term objectives throughout the negotiation. Resist getting derailed by short-term disruptions or provocations that can divert your attention from the primary goals.

- **Use Time Wisely:** Apply time pressure as both a challenge and a strategic advantage in negotiations. Harness it effectively by pacing the discussions thoughtfully, incorporating breaks as needed, and refraining from making rushed decisions that might compromise the quality of the agreement.

Adapting to New Information

A hallmark of skilled negotiation is the ability to stay flexible and adapt strategies in response to new information. Rigid adherence to a pre-set plan can be counterproductive, particularly if the situation evolves or new opportunities present themselves.

Consider a scenario where, during negotiations for a long-term supply contract, one party learns that their counterpart has adopted a more efficient production method. This revelation could lead to renegotiation on more advantageous terms, such as lower costs or enhanced delivery timelines.

Being receptive to altering your approach in light of new information can enhance negotiation outcomes and signal a readiness to collaborate, which may strengthen the relationship between the parties involved.

Creating Value in Negotiations

One of the most effective strategies in negotiation is the creation of value. This approach involves identifying and expanding the resources or benefits available to all parties, often described as 'expanding the pie.' By doing so, it addresses the interests of all involved, going beyond mere compromise to generate additional value.

Take, for instance, a negotiation between a publisher and an author. Instead of merely debating over royalty rates, they could explore other collaborative opportunities such as co-authoring a sequel, organizing joint promotional events, or creating a multimedia series. These initiatives can enhance the overall deal's value, making it more appealing to both parties.

In another example, a real estate developer was negotiating with a city government to purchase a strategically located parcel of land. The city initially insisted on a high price due to the land's prime location. Instead of fixating on the cost, the developer proposed a mixed-use project that included public parks and affordable housing, aligning with the city's urban development goals.

This approach expanded the deal's value by addressing the broader interests of the city and led to a mutually beneficial agreement. The developer acquired the land at a reasonable price, while the city benefited from a development that supported its community objectives.

The Power of Non-Verbal Communication in Negotiation

Non-verbal communication is pivotal in negotiations, often conveying more than spoken words. Elements such as body language, facial expressions, eye contact, and tone of voice significantly influence negotiation outcomes. Awareness of your non-verbal cues, along with the ability to interpret those of the other party, can provide a considerable advantage.

For instance, steady eye contact can project confidence and sincerity, enhancing trustworthiness, while crossed arms might suggest a defensive or closed stance. Conversely, a relaxed and open posture can foster rapport and trust, making the other party more open to your proposals.

Step 2: Assessment of the Other Party

In negotiations, thoroughly understanding the other party is fundamental to securing a successful outcome. This crucial step involves evaluating who the other parties are, discerning their interests and positions, and identifying their potential alternatives.

Conducting a comprehensive assessment equips negotiators with the insights needed to develop strategies that are both informed and adaptable, thereby enhancing the chances of achieving a mutually beneficial agreement.

Who Are the Other Parties?

Recognizing all the parties involved in a negotiation is not always a straightforward task. While some parties are visibly present at the negotiation table, there are often others who influence the proceedings from behind the scenes. These 'hidden parties' and 'hidden individuals' can wield considerable influence, as they often have the power to shape decisions without being directly involved in the discussions.

For example, during a labor negotiation, although the union representative is the one physically negotiating with the management team, the union members, who may not be present, ultimately have the power to approve or reject the agreement. Similarly, key decision-makers or influential advisors within an organization, who may not be physically present, also play a critical role in shaping the negotiation strategy and outcome.

Identifying these hidden parties and individuals and understanding their desires and expectations is crucial for developing a negotiation strategy that effectively addresses the needs and concerns of all involved stakeholders.

Others' Interests and Position

A critical element of negotiation involves understanding the interests and positions of the other parties. Positions represent the explicit demands or objectives that a party presents, such as a specific price or contract term. Interests, however, delve deeper, revealing the underlying motivations and reasons behind these positions as discussed earlier in this chapter. A proficient negotiator conducts thorough research to identify these interests, which can reveal pathways to common ground or opportunities to create value in the negotiation.

Consider a business negotiation where a supplier demands a higher price (position) due to increased production costs (interest). By recognizing this, the buyer could suggest a longer-term contract that ensures stability for both parties. This approach addresses the supplier's concerns and helps the buyer secure more advantageous terms.

Effective negotiation preparation involves deeply understanding the needs, interests, and motivations of the other party. This means looking beyond their initial stated positions and exploring the underlying factors that drive their decisions.

Other Negotiators' BATNA

The concept of the Best Alternative to a Negotiated Agreement (BATNA) is fundamental in negotiation. It denotes the most beneficial course of action a party can pursue if the negotiation does not conclude successfully. Understanding the other party's BATNA is just as crucial as being aware of your own. If the other party has a weak BATNA, you may possess greater leverage to negotiate more favorable terms. A strong BATNA on their side might necessitate a re-evaluation of your negotiation strategy.

A notable example involved a small technology startup in negotiations with a major corporation over licensing a new software product. The startup meticulously researched the corporation's recent financial performance, market position, and strategic goals, uncovering that the corporation faced significant pressure to innovate swiftly in the software domain to remain competitive.

Armed with this information, the startup negotiated from a position of strength, highlighting the unique benefits and strategic value of their software. This strategy resulted in a favorable licensing agreement that included a substantial upfront payment, ongoing royalties, and opportunities for future collaboration.

This scenario underscores the importance of thorough research in negotiations, illustrating how a profound understanding of the other party's situation and limitations can facilitate markedly better outcomes.

Step 3: Assessment of the Situation

After assessing yourself and the other party, it is critical to evaluate the broader context of the negotiation. This includes determining whether the negotiation is a standalone occurrence or part of an ongoing relationship. It also involves understanding the nature of the conflict and the existing power dynamics. Analyzing these elements helps tailor your negotiation strategy to the specific circumstances and can influence the approach and outcomes significantly.

Is the Negotiation Short-Term or Long-Term?

Many negotiations do not occur in isolation but within the framework of ongoing relationships. In scenarios where negotiations are frequent or continuous, the dynamics of interaction and the trust established between parties become as crucial as the immediate outcomes. Negotiators need to consider the long-term impact of their decisions on future relations and weigh whether short-term gains justify potential damage to sustained collaboration.

For example, consider a technology firm negotiating software licensing agreements with a vendor. The firm might push for significant discounts or stringent terms in the short term to reduce costs. However, pressing the vendor too hard could jeopardize the relationship, leading to less favorable support or cooperation in future updates and developments. By adopting a more balanced approach that acknowledges the vendor's need for sustainable business practices, the firm can foster a reliable long-term partnership that benefits both parties through continuous innovation and support.

Is the Negotiation One of Necessity or Opportunity?

Negotiations can arise from necessity or opportunity, each guiding the participants toward distinct objectives. Necessity-driven negotiations occur when parties need to make a deal to address urgent needs or solve critical issues. In contrast, opportunity-driven negotiations are pursued to take advantage of favorable situations to improve one's position.

For example, imagine someone who must quickly find a new job after being laid off. This necessity-driven negotiation requires swift action and may lead to compromises on salary or job role due to the urgency to secure employment and maintain financial stability.

Alternatively, consider someone who is currently employed and exploring other job opportunities without urgent need. This opportunity-driven negotiation allows the individual to negotiate from a position of strength, possibly securing better salary and benefits, as there is no immediate pressure to accept an offer.

It is crucial to understand whether a negotiation arises from necessity or opportunity as this knowledge fundamentally shapes the urgency, strategy, and adaptability required of the negotiating parties. Recognizing these underlying dynamics allows negotiators to tailor their tactics effectively, ensuring they are in harmony with the core motivations behind the negotiation.

Moreover, it is important to consider that leveraging a strong position in negotiations born out of necessity may not sustain long-term advantages. As circumstances evolve, the opposing party may seek more favorable opportunities. For instance, an employee who accepts a salary significantly below market rate due to urgent circumstances will likely pursue a more competitive compensation once the opportunity arises. This example underscores the importance of crafting negotiations that are not only responsive to immediate pressures but are also sustainable and fair in the long run.

Are Negotiations Public or Private?
The setting of a negotiation, whether public or private, plays a crucial role in shaping its process and outcomes. Public negotiations, such as those in high-profile political or corporate scenarios, often come with a level of observation and public exposure that can limit the parties' flexibility. These settings may force negotiators to adopt positions that uphold public expectations or align with broader policy stances, potentially constraining more open discussions.

Conversely, private negotiations allow for more discreet and frank exchanges, enabling parties to explore creative and mutually beneficial solutions away from the public eye. The absence of external pressures in private settings can often lead to more genuine and productive negotiations.

A classic example of the interplay between public and private negotiations can be seen in the Cuban Missile Crisis in October 1962. This high-stakes confrontation involved both public and private negotiations between the United States and the Soviet Union. Publicly, the negotiations led to the Soviets agreeing to dismantle their missile bases in Cuba in exchange for a U.S. pledge not to invade Cuba. Privately, however, a concurrent secret agreement was reached, wherein the U.S. agreed to remove its missiles from Turkey, a detail that remained classified for over 25 years.

This strategic use of both public and private negotiations played a pivotal role in defusing one of the most critical confrontations of the Cold War and preventing a potential nuclear disaster.

The Location of the Negotiation
The location of a negotiation profoundly influences the dynamics and outcomes of the discussions. It is not merely a backdrop; rather, the environment plays a critical role in shaping the psychology, comfort levels, and decisions of the involved parties. This influence encompasses both the physical setting—such as its neutrality, privacy, and symbolic value—as well as the cultural context surrounding the negotiation.

For example, choosing a neutral location can help level the playing field for all parties, mitigating any perceived or real advantages associated with negotiating on one party's "home turf." A neutral venue promotes an atmosphere of equality, ensuring that no party feels disadvantaged due to the familiarity or psychological comfort of a known or home environment.

A notable example of the strategic importance of negotiation location was the 1985 Summit in Geneva between U.S. President Ronald Reagan and Soviet General Secretary Mikhail Gorbachev. This meeting was a critical juncture in Cold War history, the first of several high-stakes discussions on international relations and the nuclear arms race.

Geneva was selected as the venue for its neutrality and historical role in hosting significant international discussions and organizations, making it an acceptable choice for both superpowers. This neutrality fostered an environment conducive to open dialogue, allowing both leaders to discuss their concerns and objectives without the psychological pressures that might have been present had the summit occurred in either the United States or the Soviet Union.

The selection of a negotiation setting is more than a logistical detail; it is a strategic decision that can significantly affect the tone, progression, and success of the negotiations. Whether seeking neutrality, capitalizing on the symbolic significance of a location, or simply looking for a space that encourages open and equitable dialogue, negotiators must thoughtfully consider the setting for their discussions.

Is there any Time Constrains?
Time constraints are a critical factor in negotiations, significantly influencing the strategies and behaviors of the parties involved. The pressure of a looming deadline can intensify the urgency to reach an

agreement, often forcing negotiators to make quicker decisions than they might under less pressured circumstances. This dynamic can work to the advantage of one party if they can manage the time pressure more effectively than the other, or if they are better prepared to handle negotiations under tight deadlines.

When time is limited, negotiators are compelled to prioritize their objectives, focusing on the most critical issues while leaving less important matters for future discussion or compromise. This can streamline the negotiation process but may also lead to rushed decisions that overlook long-term consequences or critical details. The urgency created by time constraints can sometimes result in concessions that would not have been made in a more relaxed environment.

Moreover, time constraints can create a power imbalance, where the party that can afford to wait holds a significant advantage. For instance, if one party is under significant time pressure—due to an expiring contract, an approaching deadline, or external pressures— they may feel compelled to concede to the other party's demands. Conversely, a party with no time pressure may use delays strategically, knowing that the opposing side may eventually cave under the weight of time.

A clear example of this can be seen in labor negotiations, where unions and employers often face deadlines, such as the expiration of a collective bargaining agreement or the threat of a strike. As the deadline looms, both sides feel mounting pressure to avoid a work stoppage, which can have severe financial and operational repercussions. This often forces both parties to make significant concessions in order to reach an agreement before time runs out.

In high-stakes business deals, time constraints can sometimes lead to what is known as 'deal fever,' where both parties become so focused on closing the deal within the allotted timeframe that they may overlook critical details or fail to conduct thorough due diligence. The desire to meet the deadline can overshadow the need for a careful assessment of the risks involved, potentially leading to agreements that may not serve the long-term interests of either party.

Time constraints are a powerful element in negotiations, shaping the decisions, strategies, and outcomes of the process. Negotiators must be acutely aware of the role time plays and manage it effectively—whether by pacing discussions strategically, using time pressure to their advantage, or ensuring that urgency does not lead to hasty, suboptimal decisions. Understanding and leveraging time constraints can be the key to navigating negotiations successfully, even under intense pressure.

Is the Agreement Required
When determining whether an agreement is necessary in a negotiation, the stakes and available options for each party significantly shape the strategies and tactics used. The need to reach an agreement can heavily influence the negotiation dynamics, dictating whether one party holds more leverage or whether both sides are compelled to compromise to reach a resolution.

A historical example of how the necessity of an agreement affects negotiations can be seen in the U.S. Air Traffic Controllers' strike of August 1981. When 85% of the 17,500 air traffic controllers went on strike, they violated a 1947 law that forbade strikes by government employees. President Ronald Reagan ordered the striking workers to return within 48 hours or face termination. While the controllers viewed an agreement as essential to improving working conditions, the government did not feel compelled to negotiate under the terms presented, believing they could continue operations without the striking workers. This resulted in over 5,000 controllers receiving dismissal notices, illustrating how the perceived necessity—or lack thereof—of an agreement can drastically alter negotiation outcomes.

This example highlights the importance of assessing whether an agreement is required and by whom. Understanding this dynamic allows negotiators to strategically approach discussions, recognizing when they can push for better terms or when they must prioritize a swift resolution. The ability—or inability—to walk away can greatly influence the direction and outcome of any negotiation.

Is Ratification Required?
In complex negotiations, the need for ratification—approval from a higher authority or governing body—can be a decisive factor in the success of an agreement. Ratification often adds an additional layer to the negotiation process, as the agreement reached at the table may need approval before it becomes legally binding.

For instance, consider a hiring manager negotiating terms with a candidate. While the manager might have authority to discuss salary and benefits, the final offer may need approval from the human resources department to ensure it aligns with company policies and budgets. Without ratification, the agreement would not be final or enforceable. Similarly, in government contract negotiations, agreements might require ratification from a city council or regulatory body to ensure they comply with broader public policies and legal requirements.

Understanding the requirement for ratification is essential for negotiators, as it influences both strategic planning and implementation timelines. Negotiators must be aware of the limits of their authority at the table and anticipate potential changes that may arise during the ratification process. Aligning with the interests of those responsible for ratification is critical to ensuring that agreements are ultimately approved and successfully implemented.

Do Agreements have to be Official?

The formality of an agreement can vary depending on the context, stakes, and relationship between the parties involved. In some negotiations, formal contracts are necessary to legally bind parties to fulfill their promises. These contracts often include detailed terms, timelines, and consequences for non-compliance, which is common in business transactions, employment negotiations, and large-scale projects.

For example, in salary negotiations, a formal contract may outline the details of a salary increase, including the amount, start date, and conditions. This legally binding document ensures that both parties are clear on the terms, reducing the likelihood of disputes.

However, not all agreements are formalized with contracts. In some cases, deals are made through informal means, such as a handshake, which relies on trust and goodwill between the parties. While a handshake can symbolize commitment, it lacks the legal enforceability of a written contract, which can lead to complications if one party fails to honor the agreement.

A famous example of an informal agreement that backfired is the McDonald's handshake deal. In the 1950s, Ray Kroc partnered with

Richard and Maurice McDonald to franchise their restaurant business. In 1961, Kroc agreed to buy out the brothers for $2.7 million and reportedly promised a 1% royalty on future profits through a handshake deal. However, this informal agreement was never honored, and the McDonald brothers missed out on what could have been a fortune in royalties.

This case serves as a cautionary tale about the risks of informal agreements. While handshakes can signify trust, they leave parties vulnerable if expectations are not formalized. The McDonald brothers' story underscores the importance of formalizing agreements to protect one's interests, especially in high-stakes business dealings.

Cultural Considerations in Negotiation

In international negotiations or when dealing with parties from different cultural backgrounds, understanding cultural norms and values is essential. Cultural differences can significantly impact communication styles, decision-making processes, and expectations in negotiations. Failing to recognize these details can lead to misunderstandings, conflicts, or missed opportunities.

For example, some cultures prioritize building personal relationships before engaging in business discussions, while others may prefer a more direct approach. Additionally, concepts of time, authority, and negotiation strategies can vary widely. Being aware of and respecting these differences fosters trust and promotes smoother negotiations.

A relevant case involved a U.S. company negotiating a joint venture with a Japanese firm. The U.S. team, accustomed to fast-paced and direct negotiations, initially struggled with the more reserved and consensus-driven approach of their Japanese counterparts. Recognizing the importance of cultural sensitivity, the U.S. negotiators adjusted their strategy, allowing more time for discussions and relationship-building. This shift in approach led to a successful joint venture, as both parties aligned their expectations and collaborated effectively. This example highlights the importance of cultural awareness and adapting negotiation strategies to fit the cultural context.

Understanding Power Dynamics in Negotiations

Power dynamics play a crucial role in negotiations. The balance of power between the parties can influence the negotiation process and outcomes significantly. Power in negotiation can come from various sources, such as expertise, control over resources, or the ability to walk away from the deal.

It is important to recognize when you have the upper hand in a negotiation and when you might be at a disadvantage. However, having power does not necessarily mean using it aggressively. In fact, those with more power can often achieve better long-term results by using their power to create fair and balanced agreements.

For example, a supplier with a unique product that a buyer needs might have significant power in the negotiation. However, if the supplier uses this power to demand unreasonable terms, it could damage the relationship and future business opportunities. Instead, the supplier could use their power to negotiate favorable terms while still ensuring that the buyer feels valued and respected.

Direct vs. Indirect Negotiation in Conflict Situations

In conflict situations, such as wars or major disputes, direct negotiations between parties may be unfeasible due to security, political, or logistical challenges. In such cases, negotiations often proceed indirectly through third-party mediators. These mediators, who can be jointly selected by both negotiating parties, typically represent neutral organizations or, in the case of political conflicts, countries uninvolved in the dispute. Their primary role is to facilitate communication by relaying messages, proposals, and responses between the conflicting sides.

The success of indirect negotiations largely depends on the neutrality and perceived impartiality of the mediators. When mediators are chosen by both parties, it ensures a level of trust in their ability to fairly represent each side's concerns. This impartiality is critical for maintaining balance in the negotiation and fostering an environment conducive to dialogue.

Effective mediation involves more than just relaying information; it requires building trust, accurately conveying positions, and identifying common interests that can lead to mutually acceptable solutions. Mediators may also implement confidence-building measures early in the process to show the benefits of cooperation, encouraging further engagement.

Building Trust in Negotiation

Trust is a cornerstone of successful negotiations, particularly in long-term relationships or complex deals. Building trust involves demonstrating reliability, transparency, and a genuine commitment to finding mutually beneficial solutions.

A keyway to foster trust is through consistent and open communication. Sharing relevant information, being honest about your intentions, and following through on promises can establish credibility and create a cooperative atmosphere. For instance, in a partnership negotiation, one party can build trust by being transparent about their financial situation, reassuring the other side that they are negotiating in good faith. This trust can lead to more collaborative discussions and better outcomes for both parties.

In one example, a manufacturing company was negotiating a long-term supply agreement with a key supplier. To build trust, the company invited the supplier's management team to visit their facilities and meet with key personnel. They also shared detailed forecasts and plans for future growth, showcasing their commitment to a long-term partnership. This transparency helped lay a strong foundation of trust, enabling both sides to negotiate more effectively. The supplier gained confidence in the company's reliability, while the company secured favorable terms and ensured a stable supply chain.

Summary

Negotiation is a multifaceted and dynamic process that goes beyond simply reaching an agreement; it requires a profound understanding of the strategies and principles that lead to successful outcomes. Throughout this chapter, we have explored the core elements of effective negotiation, with particular emphasis on the pivotal role that preparation plays. Preparation is not just a preliminary step but the cornerstone upon which successful negotiations are built. It encompasses three key areas: self-assessment, assessment of the other party, and assessment of the broader situation.

Self-assessment is vital for ensuring that negotiators enter discussions with a clear sense of their objectives, boundaries, and emotional triggers. This introspective process allows individuals to understand their priorities—what they are willing to compromise and what they are determined to achieve. It also prepares them to manage their emotional responses during the negotiation, avoiding decisions driven by pressure or stress.

The assessment of the other party is equally crucial. It involves researching and analyzing the other side's interests, positions, and potential alternatives. This insight helps negotiators uncover opportunities for collaboration and provides leverage when negotiating. Understanding the other party's motivations enables negotiators to tailor their proposals in ways that appeal to the other side, ultimately facilitating a more cooperative and productive negotiation process.

The third cornerstone of robust preparation is a thorough situation assessment. This comprehensive analysis encompasses the exploration of power dynamics, cultural influences, and external pressures that may influence the negotiation process. Factors such as time constraints, the imperative of securing an agreement, and the involvement of external stakeholders, including ratifying entities, are critical to understand. Gaining insight into these aspects enables negotiators to strategically overcome challenges and leverage opportunities effectively. Additionally, it equips them to modify their strategies adaptively as new information emerges or circumstances evolve throughout the negotiation.

In conclusion, the importance of preparation in negotiation cannot be overstated. Preparation provides the foundation upon which successful negotiations are built, empowering negotiators to approach discussions with confidence, adaptability, and a clear strategy. By thoroughly assessing themselves, the other party, and the broader situation, negotiators are better equipped to create value, build trust, and secure mutually beneficial agreements. Whether in high-stakes business deals, political negotiations, or everyday disputes, the ability to prepare effectively is often the key to achieving successful outcomes in any negotiation.

Chapter Six

Problem-Solving and Decision-Making

T he ability to solve problems and make effective decisions is fundamental to achieving success in both personal and professional contexts. Whether navigating the complexities of a corporate environment, managing a team, or handling day-to-day challenges, problem-solving and decision-making skills are essential for overcoming obstacles and seizing opportunities.

In this chapter, we explore structured processes that lead to effective problem-solving and decision-making. We will examine the key steps, from accurately defining a problem to monitoring the implementation of the chosen solution. Along the way, we will introduce proven techniques like the 5 Whys, SMART objectives, and decision-making models, offering a solid framework for tackling complex issues.

Through a combination of theory and practical examples, this chapter aims to equip you with the tools needed to approach problems systematically and make informed decisions. Whether you are facing a critical business decision or a personal dilemma, the principles outlined here will help you navigate the process with confidence and clarity.

A problem arises when there is a gap between the current state and the desired state. For instance, if a team is consistently missing project deadlines, the problem lies in the difference between actual performance and expected outcomes.

Problems can be classified into three categories:

Problems that have already occurred: These issues require immediate attention, such as a machine breakdown in a factory that halts production.

Problems that lie ahead: These are potential challenges that can be mitigated with proactive measures. For example, multinational company once anticipated a supply chain disruption due to global political tensions. To avoid delays, they diversified their suppliers and maintained production schedules despite the challenges.

Problems you want to prevent: These potential issues have not yet occurred, but they are mitigated through preventative measures. Examples include implementing cybersecurity protocols to prevent data breaches, adopting business continuity management (BCM) strategies, and establishing disaster recovery (DR) plans to ensure rapid response and restoration of operations in the event of a major disruption.

Effective problem-solving and decision-making involves a systematic approach, which includes the following six steps (Figure 17):

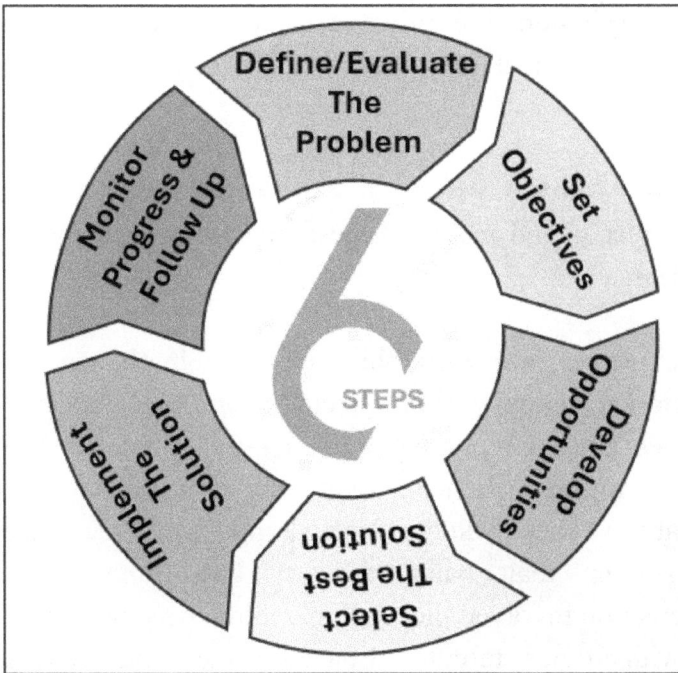

Figure 17. Six Steps of Problem-Solving and Decision-Making

Step 1 – Define and Evaluate the Problem: Clearly identifying the issue is the foundation for finding an effective solution.

Step 2 – Set Objectives: Establishing goals guides the decision-making process.

Step 3 – Develop Opportunities: Brainstorming possible solutions provides a range of options to consider.

Step 4 – Select the Best Solution: Evaluating the pros and cons of each option helps determine the most effective course of action.

Step 5 – Implement the Solution: Careful planning and resource allocation are critical to ensure the chosen solution is executed properly.

Step 6 – Monitor Progress and Follow Up: Continuously assessing results and making necessary adjustments ensures long-term success.

For example, a mid-sized financial firm implemented a new information technology (IT) system to enhance data processing capabilities. After defining the problem—their outdated system was slowing operations—the team set objectives to improve efficiency and scalability. They evaluated several options and selected a cloud-based system that balanced cost and functionality. The implementation involved thorough planning, training, and a phased rollout, with progress monitored and adjustments made as necessary. Ultimately, the new system greatly improved the firm's operational efficiency.

Problem-solving and decision-making are critical skills that can determine the success or failure of any endeavor. By understanding the nature of problems, applying a structured decision-making process, and learning from real-world examples, individuals and organizations can navigate challenges more effectively.

Now, let us delve into the six essential steps of problem-solving and decision-making. Each step is designed to guide you through identifying, analyzing, and resolving issues effectively, ensuring thorough and considered outcomes.

Step 1: Define and Evaluate the Problem

Defining and evaluating a problem is the critical initial step in any problem-solving process. This phase involves accurately identifying the discrepancy between the current situation and the desired outcome. A precise understanding of the problem is essential for devising an effective solution and is fundamental across various contexts, including technical, business, and personal environments. Neglecting to recognize or inaccurately defining a problem can worsen issues and lead to ineffective solutions.

In a corporate setting, if projects are consistently missing deadlines, it is crucial to clearly define the problem. Is it due to inadequate resource allocation, unrealistic timelines, or a lack of communication among team members? Similarly, in a personal context, if an individual experiences ongoing fatigue, determining the root cause—be it poor sleep habits, a medical condition, or excessive stress—is essential for finding the right intervention.

Symptoms vs. Causes

A key component of problem definition, regardless of context, is distinguishing between symptoms and causes. Symptoms are the observable indicators of an issue, while causes are the deeper underlying factors. Merely addressing symptoms can provide temporary relief; however, without resolving the root causes, the problems may recur, potentially in worse forms.

This principle applies universally, whether dealing with personal health, workplace conflicts, societal issues, or political unrest. For example, treating only the symptoms of a health problem, like using

149

pain relief for chronic headaches, without addressing underlying high blood pressure, offers only short-term relief and can lead to serious complications. Similarly, in a professional context, a company facing customer dissatisfaction might see unhappy customers as a direct symptom. However, the root cause might be inadequate employee training leading to poor service. Systematically addressing this root issue—rather than offering superficial compensations—prevents future dissatisfaction.

Implementing structured techniques and methodologies is crucial for identifying the underlying causes of problems rather than merely addressing their symptoms. Tools such as the 5 Whys Technique, the Fishbone Diagram, and Cause Mapping allow organizations and individuals to systematically dissect a problem to its core components.

This approach ensures that solutions are not just superficial fixes but are targeted at the root causes, thereby preventing recurrence of the issue and leading to more sustainable outcomes. These methods encourage a thorough examination of all contributing factors, fostering a deeper understanding of the problem and facilitating the development of more effective and enduring solutions.

The 5 Whys Technique

This technique is employed to delve into the cause-and-effect relationships that underpin a problem. By iteratively asking 'why' a problem occurs (Figure 18), deeper layers of causation are uncovered, often revealing insights that go beyond the obvious initial answers. It is important to note that the name '5 Whys' does not restrict the inquiry to exactly five questions; the number of 'whys' can be fewer or more, depending on the specific case and the depth of the underlying issues.

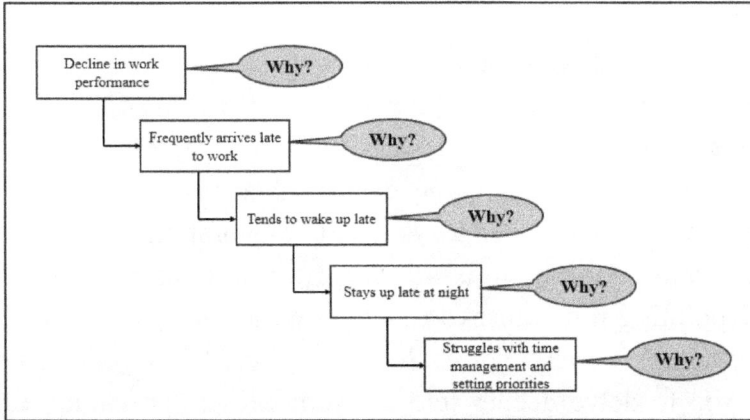

Figure 18. 5 Whys Technique

A notable application of the '5 Whys' technique was used to understand the deterioration of the Washington Monument. The initial problem identified was damage from harsh cleaning chemicals. The application of the '5 Whys' revealed that the lights being turned on early in the evening attracted gnats, which in turn attracted spiders, then birds, whose droppings made frequent cleaning necessary. The simple solution—delaying the lighting— mitigated the need for harsh chemicals.

Similarly, in the medical field, consider a patient who frequently experiences headaches. If a doctor prescribes pain relief pills, this may temporarily alleviate the headache but does not address the underlying cause. Employing the '5 Whys' technique might reveal that the patient is not getting enough sleep, or further investigation could uncover more serious issues like high blood pressure.

Understanding these root causes enables more effective and lasting treatments to be implemented, such as lifestyle adjustments or medical interventions specific to the underlying condition.

Fishbone Diagram Method (Ishikawa)

The Fishbone Diagram, also known as the cause and effect diagram or the Ishikawa Diagram (refer to Figure 19), serves as a powerful visual tool for organizing the causes of a problem into distinct categories. This facilitates a systematic exploration of all potential factors contributing to an issue. The diagram is particularly useful for pinpointing root causes in areas such as Methods, Machinery, People, and Materials. For each category, the "5 Whys" method is employed to delve deeper into the root causes, providing a clear pathway to uncover underlying issues. Furthermore, the analysis can be extended to even more detailed levels as necessary to thoroughly address and resolve the problem.

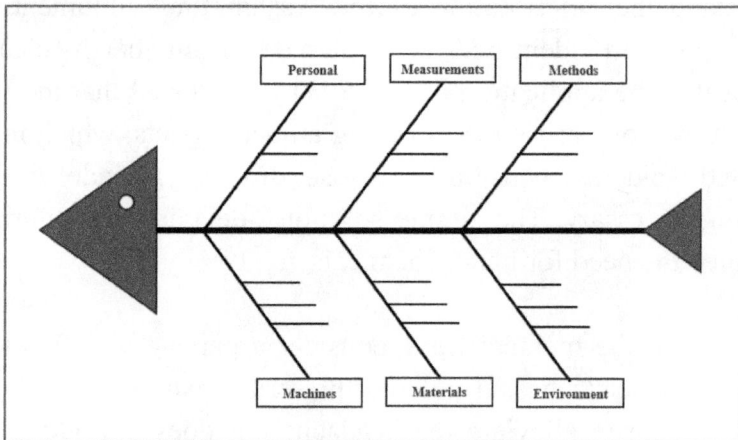

Figure 19. Fishbone Diagram

For instance, in a restaurant delivery service experiencing ongoing delays, the Fishbone Diagram can be instrumental in effectively identifying and categorizing the root causes of the problem. These causes can typically be grouped into major categories such as:

- **People**: Challenges may include inadequate training and high employee turnover.

- **Methods**: Inefficient delivery routing strategies, such as failure to utilize advanced GPS systems for navigation.

- **Machinery**: Poor maintenance of delivery vehicles, leading to frequent breakdowns and service interruptions.

- **Materials**: Inconsistent supply of ingredients, which delays food preparation and reduces overall efficiency.

However, the real value of the Fishbone Diagram lies in drilling down into second, third, or even deeper levels of each category, moving beyond surface-level symptoms. For example, exploring the root causes of high employee turnover may reveal underlying issues such as uncompetitive wages, lack of team cohesion, or poor recruitment practices. A further layer of analysis might uncover organizational inefficiencies, weak managerial oversight, or financial constraints contributing to these issues.

By applying this structured and iterative approach, organizations can uncover the deeper, often hidden causes of operational challenges. This leads to more effective, long-term solutions that address the core problems and ultimately result in improved service performance.

Cause Mapping Method

Employing the 5 Whys technique, this method offers a detailed visual representation of cause-and-effect relationships using a logical structure, enhancing problem-solving by detailing every contributing factor and their interconnections (Figure 20).

The sinking of the Titanic, for example, has been analyzed using Cause Mapping to identify contributing factors such as insufficient lifeboats, inadequate lookout procedures, and the collision with an iceberg. The analysis also examined deeper systemic issues, including flawed safety standards and poor emergency preparedness, offering comprehensive insights into both the specific incident and broader safety protocols.

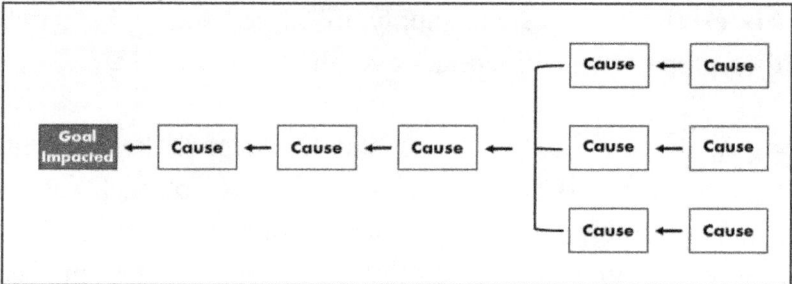

Figure 20. Cause Mapping Method

Evaluating and Articulating the Problem

Accurate problem identification requires critical thinking and analytical skills to articulate a clear, concise problem statement, setting the foundation for the problem-solving process. For example, rather than a vague 'Sales are declining,' a precise statement might specify, 'Sales in the northeast region have declined by 15% over the

154

last two quarters due to increased competition and customer dissatisfaction.'

Once the problem is identified, evaluating it involves gathering data, understanding the context, and considering all potential factors. Whether in a business setting or personal scenario, this comprehensive understanding of symptoms versus causes is crucial. Effective resolution requires digging deeper to address the root cause, leading to sustainable solutions and preventing future issues.

Step 2: Set Objectives

Setting objectives is a critical step in both problem-solving and decision-making. This step determines what needs to be achieved, prioritize actions, allocate resources effectively, and understand any constraints. By clearly defining objectives, individuals and teams can focus their efforts on shared goals, ensuring that every action is purpose-driven and aligned with broader targets. These objectives serve as key markers for planning and execution, essential in contexts as diverse as corporate projects and personal growth.

Implementing SMART Objectives

As previously addressed in Chapter One, 'Time Management: Stay Focused,' and reiterated here for clarity, it is essential that objectives be precisely formulated utilizing the SMART criteria—Specific, Measurable, Attainable, Relevant, and Time-bound. Each component of this acronym is crucial in developing objectives that are clear, actionable, and strategically aligned with broader goals:

- **Specific**: Clear and unambiguous objectives provide a definitive direction and facilitate focused efforts. For instance, rather than a general goal like "enhance customer satisfaction," a more specific objective would detail the actions and expected outcomes, such as "increase customer satisfaction scores from 3.5 to 4.2 out of 5 by improving call center response times and training staff in customer engagement techniques over the next year."

- **Measurable**: Objectives must have concrete criteria for measuring progress and outcomes. This allows for the objective assessment of whether targets are being met and facilitates necessary adjustments. For example, a measurable objective could be "reduce manufacturing defects by 25% within the next six months through enhanced quality control procedures and staff training."

- **Attainable**: Objectives should be realistically achievable given the available resources, capabilities, and time. They should challenge the team but remain feasible to keep morale high and ensure commitment. An unrealistic goal, such as "increase market share by 50% in a saturated market within three months," might set the stage for failure.

- **Relevant**: Each objective should directly support the broader strategic goals of the organization or align with individual growth aspirations. This relevance ensures that the efforts contribute positively to the overall mission, like a software company aiming to "secure three new enterprise clients in the Northeast region by the end of the fiscal year to expand market presence."

- **Time-bound**: Setting a deadline for objectives creates urgency and prioritizes efforts. Time-bound goals help manage and pace the workload, such as "launch the new online marketing campaign by the end of Q2 to capitalize on the peak shopping season."

Consider a retail business experiencing a downturn in sales. By setting SMART objectives, the management can strategically address this challenge. A specific and measurable goal would be, "Increase in-store sales by 15% over the next quarter by deploying targeted marketing strategies and optimizing the product mix." This goal is attainable with the right marketing and product strategies, relevant to the business's aim to improve financial performance, and time-bound with a clear quarterly deadline.

It is crucial for a goal to meet all the elements of the SMART framework to be considered well-constructed. Failure to meet even one element can lead to a goal that is less actionable and potentially unachievable.

- **Example of a broad and vague goal**: "Expand business operations" is a goal that lacks specificity and measurability. Without details on how or where the business should expand, or clear metrics for expansion, the goal is too ambiguous to be actionable. Moreover, without a timeframe that reflects realistic strategic growth, such a goal could lead to resource misallocation and strategic missteps.

- **Example of an overly ambitious goal**: "Dominate the global market in one year" might not only be unattainable but also irrelevant if the company lacks the resources or global presence necessary for such expansion.

The Power of Well-Defined Objectives

Adhering to the SMART criteria transforms objectives from mere aspirations into powerful, actionable plans. This structured approach to setting objectives ensures clarity, manageability, and alignment with broader strategic aims. Whether implemented in corporate environments, educational institutions, or personal projects, SMART objectives provide a clear framework for focused action and measurable success. By effectively guiding problem-solving and decision-making processes, they help ensure significant and meaningful outcomes are achieved.

Step 3: Develop Opportunities

In the problem-solving and decision-making process, developing opportunities is a pivotal step. It involves identifying and exploring various potential solutions, thereby expanding the scope beyond a single approach. This critical stage enables teams to explore multiple avenues for resolving the issue, ensuring a comprehensive evaluation of possible solutions. This thorough exploration enhances the likelihood of selecting the most effective and sustainable outcome. Further details on the selection process will be discussed in Step Four of the problem-solving and decision-making process.

The process of developing opportunities is markedly effective when it incorporates a wide array of perspectives. Engaging team members, subject matter experts, and external stakeholders enriches the ideation pool significantly. Such collaboration is instrumental in driving creativity and innovation, as diverse viewpoints often lead to unique solution pathways that might not surface in a more homogenous group.

Optimizing Brainstorming Sessions

Brainstorming is a cornerstone technique for generating diverse solutions. To maximize the efficacy of these sessions, it is crucial to foster an environment where all participants feel comfortable sharing their ideas, regardless of how unconventional they may appear.

A key strategy for successful brainstorming is to suspend judgment during the initial idea-generation phase. This approach encourages free thinking and broad participation, which often leads to synergistic outcomes. When team members build on each other's ideas, the collective creativity can exceed the sum of individual contributions, leading to innovative solutions that might not emerge in a more restrictive setting.

For example, a retail company addressing customer service complaints implemented brainstorming sessions across various company levels. Ideas such as establishing a 'Customer Experience Task Force' and launching a 'Customer Appreciation Day' emerged. These initiatives, derived from cross-departmental inputs, significantly enhanced customer satisfaction and reduced complaint rates.

The inclusion of varied perspectives is not just beneficial but essential in developing a broad spectrum of viable solutions.

Participants from different backgrounds and expertise contribute to a richer dialogue, unveiling opportunities that may remain hidden in more homogeneous groups.

An illustrative case involves a nonprofit looking to expand its outreach. By including staff, volunteers, beneficiaries, and community leaders in the brainstorming process, the organization discovered innovative service delivery models like mobile units for underserved areas, which traditional planning might not have considered.

Balancing Creativity and Critical Thinking

Creativity is essential in developing opportunities, pushing boundaries to think outside the box and envision solutions that may not be immediately apparent. However, for creativity to be truly effective, it must be paired with critical thinking later, which assesses the feasibility and potential impacts of each idea.

For example, during a brainstorming session, a team might come up with a broad spectrum of creative solutions. What follows is a crucial phase of critical evaluation, where these ideas are scrutinized for practicality, cost-effectiveness, and resource allocation. This balanced approach ensures that the final solution is innovative, viable, and executable.

At a manufacturing plant experiencing frequent production delays, management decided to engage employees directly to foster innovative solutions. Workers were encouraged to contribute their insights and suggest improvements to the production process. Through a series of brainstorming sessions, they identified several bottlenecks and proposed practical changes to the workflow, such as rearranging the assembly line to minimize the time spent transferring parts and introducing a new quality check early in the process to detect defects sooner.

These initiatives, driven by employee input, alleviated production delays and significantly boosted morale and workplace satisfaction. Empowering employees to take ownership of problem-solving processes led to meaningful improvements in both efficiency and productivity.

Developing opportunities is a dynamic step in the problem-solving and decision-making process. It involves generating a diverse array of potential solutions, fostering collaboration, and integrating both creativity and critical thinking. By engaging a variety of participants and maintaining an open, innovative environment, organizations can craft effective solutions to complex challenges. This section has showcased the transformative power of combining collaborative creativity with strategic analysis to achieve successful outcomes.

Moreover, developing opportunities is a creative endeavor that requires looking beyond conventional solutions. It entails exploring alternative pathways and adopting different perspectives, which is crucial for uncovering innovative solutions that might not be initially obvious.

Creativity in this context is not limited to generating unique ideas; it also involves approaching problems from various angles and considering unconventional but potentially effective solutions.

161

"Aha" moments, often experienced as sudden insights or breakthroughs, are pivotal in the creative process. These instances occur when seemingly unrelated concepts connect in new and unexpected ways, typically following a period of deep reflection or challenge. Such moments are not merely products of chance; they arise from environments that nurture curiosity, encourage experimentation, and support the freedom to explore ideas without the fear of failure.

Routine activities that facilitate mental wandering often serve as catalysts for enlightening experiences. Walking, whether through the dynamic streets of a city or the serene paths of a park, provides a change of scenery and a steady rhythm that aids in organizing thoughts, often igniting significant insights. Similarly, the peaceful setting of a bathroom shower—commonly referred to as the source of "Shower Thoughts"—promotes uninterrupted subconscious thought processing, yielding surprising realizations.

Another well-known strategy is the classic "let me sleep on it" approach, where individuals distance themselves from a problem temporarily. This allows the mind to work through the issue subconsciously, often leading to a fresh perspective or solution upon waking.

By creating spaces and opportunities that allow these moments of clarity to flourish, organizations and educators can help individuals and teams transcend traditional thinking and discover groundbreaking solutions that redefine challenges and expand possibilities.

Step 4: Select the Best Solution

Choosing the best solution within the decision-making process involves a deep and careful evaluation of alternatives based on their feasibility, costs, impact, and potential consequences. Using robust, data-driven criteria ensures the chosen solution aligns with the organization's strategic goals.

In the decision-making process, employing both quantitative and qualitative data is essential for an objective comparison of options, helping to mitigate biases. For instance, a publishing company deliberating on new digital marketing strategies may analyze data from past marketing campaigns, audience engagement metrics, and projected return on investment to determine the most effective approach.

Applying Decision-Making Models

Structured decision-making models can streamline the process of selecting the most appropriate solution. Below, we explore various models through practical examples:

Pareto Analysis in Resource Allocation

Pareto Analysis leverages the 80/20 rule to concentrate resources on the most impactful issues. For instance, consider the application of this principle in the restaurant industry. As illustrated in Figure 21, the majority of customer complaints are concentrated in a few key areas, particularly complaints about meals being overpriced and unsatisfactory food portions. These two categories alone might represent the most significant share of dissatisfaction among patrons.

163

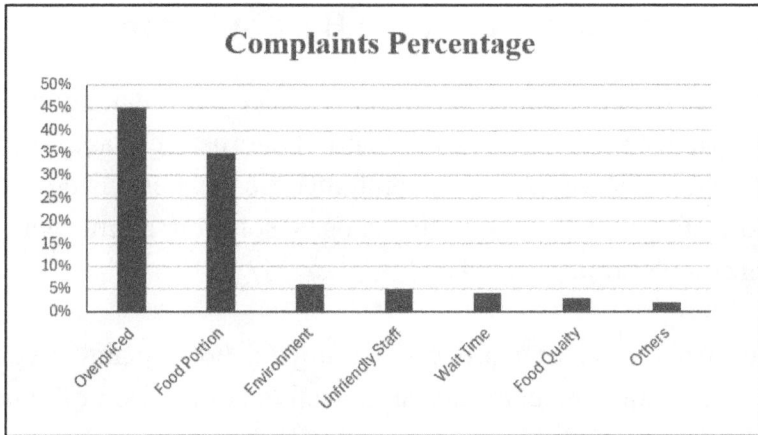

Figure 21. Sample of Complaints in a Restaurant Business

By addressing these critical issues—overpriced menu items and inadequate food portions—the management can significantly improve customer satisfaction. Focusing on these high-priority areas aligns with Pareto's principle and ensures that efforts are directed where they can have the most substantial impact on the overall customer experience.

Minimax Strategy in Managing Risks

The Minimax strategy focuses on minimizing the maximum potential loss in a worst-case scenario, making it especially useful in risk management. A notable example occurred in 1994 when Intel Corporation discovered a floating-point division error in its Pentium processors. Initially reluctant to recall the chips, Intel faced mounting public pressure and the risk of severe long-term damage to its reputation. Ultimately, the company decided to recall all defective processors at an estimated cost of $475 million. While costly in the short term, this move helped avert potentially greater losses in customer trust and preserved the company's long-term market position.

Paired Comparison Analysis

The Paired Comparison Chart (PCC) is a strategic tool used to evaluate multiple options against each other, aiding in the prioritization based on selected criteria. Consider an IT company faced with choosing its next major investment from options such as cybersecurity enhancements, cloud storage upgrades, or new Customer Relationship Management (CRM) software.

Using a Paired Comparison Chart (Figure 22), decision-makers systematically compare each investment option across various criteria, including impact on operational efficiency, cost, return on investment (ROI), and strategic alignment. This method of analysis could reveal, for instance, that cybersecurity enhancements offer the greatest benefits in terms of risk reduction and regulatory compliance, thus becoming the preferred investment choice.

	Cybersecurity	Cloud Storage	CRM Software	Total
Cybersecurity	----	1	1	2
Cloud Storage	0	----	1	1
CRM Software	0	0	----	0

Figure 22. Sample of Paired Comparison Chart

Six Thinking Hats Method

The Six Thinking Hats method, devised by Edward de Bono, promotes a structured approach to decision-making by examining issues from six distinct perspectives. This methodology ensures a thorough and comprehensive analysis, enabling participants to systematically address challenges one at a time.

By separating thinking styles, the Six Hats method enhances clarity and understanding among participants, streamlining the process of reaching a consensus or identifying the optimal solution while minimizing the risk of overlooking critical aspects.

For example, when a university administration evaluates the feasibility of launching an online learning platform, applying the Six Thinking Hats method provides a framework for thorough and balanced assessment:

White Hat (information-focused): They gather data on student technology access and the success rates of similar initiatives.

Red Hat (emotions-focused): They consider student and faculty feelings about online learning, focusing on anxieties or excitement.

Black Hat (critical-focused): They identify potential problems like technological barriers or decreased student engagement.

Yellow Hat (optimism-focused): They explore the potential benefits, such as increased flexibility and access to education.

Green Hat (creative-focused): They brainstorm innovative ways to enhance online engagement through gamification and interactive elements.

Blue Hat (process-focused): They plan the implementation phases, set timelines, and determine necessary resources.

By using the Six Hats, every dimension of the proposal is explored, ensuring that the decision is robust, well-considered, and optimally structured.

Cost-Benefit Analysis

Cost-Benefit Analysis is crucial for weighing the financial inputs against the expected benefits to ensure economic viability. A city council evaluates the construction of a new public library. The cost-benefit analysis compares initial and ongoing expenses such as construction, staffing, and maintenance with potential gains, including community educational enrichment, increased property values, and job creation. The analysis indicates that the long-term community and economic benefits substantially exceed the initial and recurring costs, strongly supporting the project's approval.

Selecting the best solution is a crucial aspect of the problem-solving and decision-making process. It involves a systematic evaluation of all viable alternatives to ensure that the final choice is effective and aligns with the organization's broader strategic goals. This step requires the use of data-driven decision-making and the application of various decision-making models to thoroughly assess each option's feasibility, cost, impact, and potential consequences.

By utilizing both quantitative and qualitative data, organizations can objectively compare alternatives, thus reducing biases and enhancing the quality of decision-making. This approach ensures that the decision-making process is not just about selecting the most immediate solution but about making strategic decisions that will have a long-lasting impact.

The final decision, derived from these rigorous methodologies, is more likely to be robust, sustainable, and capable of driving significant positive change within the organization. The methodologies and tools discussed provide a comprehensive framework that aids organizations in navigating complex decision landscapes, ensuring that every decision contributes positively towards achieving overarching strategic objectives.

Step 5: Implement the Solution

Implementing the solution is a critical phase in the problem-solving and decision-making process, where strategic ideas become actionable steps. This stage requires meticulous planning to ensure effective execution. It involves developing a comprehensive action plan, allocating appropriate resources, setting clear timelines, and designating responsibilities.

Project Management in Implementation

Effective project management is foundational to successful implementation. It converts strategic decisions into operational actions that achieve tangible results. The implementation phase demands precise planning, resource management, time scheduling, and proactive communication to facilitate smooth execution. A well-devised project plan acts as a roadmap, guiding the team from the initial stages through to successful completion.

For instance, consider a large manufacturing company implementing a new Enterprise Resource Planning (ERP) system. The effectiveness of this system integration, which spans across finance, supply chain management, and human resources, relies heavily on the meticulous management of the implementation process.

Defining Project Scope and Objectives

The initial step in project management involves defining the scope and objectives of the project. In the example of the ERP system implementation, the scope typically includes selecting appropriate ERP software, customizing it to address specific operational requirements, migrating data from legacy systems, training staff, and ensuring the system is integrated throughout the organization. The objectives might encompass improving operational efficiency by 30%, reducing operational costs, and enhancing data accuracy across the company.

Developing a Detailed Action Plan

Subsequently, the project management team develops an action plan that specifies each implementation phase. Tasks such as ERP vendor selection, system configuration, data migration, and employee training are clearly outlined and assigned to specific teams or departments with set deadlines. For example, the IT department might handle the technical setup and integration, while the HR department manages training programs.

Allocating Resources and Setting a Timeline

Resource allocation is critical for the project's success. The company must ensure sufficient financial, human, and technological resources are available to support each phase of the implementation. A realistic timeline, sensitive to the project's complexity and resource availability, is crucial. This might include milestones such as completing software setup within three months and achieving full system launch by the sixth month.

Utilizing Project Management Tools

To ensure effective control over project timelines and deliverables, tools such as Gantt charts and critical path analysis are essential for scheduling and task prioritization. Equally important is integrating robust risk management strategies that not only identify potential issues but also align each risk with appropriate mitigation measures. These measures should be evaluated in terms of time and cost impact, enabling project teams to make informed decisions that balance risk reduction with resource efficiency. This approach enhances project resilience and helps avoid costly delays.

Addressing Resistance to Change

Implementing significant changes, such as a new ERP system, often encounters resistance from employees who are accustomed to existing workflows. Effective change management strategies are crucial and focus on the human aspects of management. These strategies should involve steps to educate, engage, and empower employees throughout the transition. Measures might include comprehensive training, regular updates about the benefits of the new system, and establishing a support desk for ongoing assistance. Utilizing these change management methods ensures that the team is fully supportive once the implementation is complete.

Implementing the solution effectively is as crucial as the decision-making process itself. Through disciplined project management, clear communication, and adaptive strategies, organizations can ensure that the solutions achieve their intended goals and integrate seamlessly into existing operations, leading to sustained improvements and efficiencies.

Step 6: Monitor Progress and Follow Up

Monitoring progress is a vital step in the problem-solving and decision-making process, as it ensures that the implemented solution effectively addresses the initial problem and continues to do so over time. This step involves establishing performance measures and setting up checkpoints to assess the solution's ongoing effectiveness.

Setting Performance Measures

Performance measures are essential for assessing whether the implemented solution is achieving the goals established in Step 2 of the process. These measures may include benchmarks, customer satisfaction scores, efficiency metrics, and other relevant key performance indicators (KPIs). Regular assessment of these metrics allows organizations to identify areas for improvement and to make necessary adjustments promptly.

Continuous improvement should be a fundamental aspect of any organization's strategy. It encourages a proactive stance on refining and enhancing solutions, ensuring they remain relevant and effective. For example, a tech company that launches a new app feature would monitor user engagement and functionality issues. Initial data might show increased user interaction, but feedback could point to user interface complexities. By continuously refining the feature based on user feedback and usage data, the company can enhance the app's overall usability and effectiveness.

In the retail sector, a company might introduce a new online ordering system aimed at improving customer purchase experiences. Key performance indicators could include website traffic, conversion rates, and customer feedback on the checkout process. Suppose initial reviews indicate that customers find the checkout process confusing. In that case, the company can swiftly make interface adjustments to simplify navigation, directly addressing the feedback and improving the user experience.

Similarly, in healthcare, after implementing a new electronic health records system, a hospital may monitor various metrics such as patient wait times, the speed of data retrieval, and staff satisfaction with the new system. Continuous monitoring might reveal that data retrieval speeds are slower than expected, impacting patient wait times. The hospital can respond by upgrading hardware or optimizing software configurations to improve system performance and, consequently, patient service.

The Role of Feedback in Effective Follow-Up

Feedback is pivotal in the follow-up process, offering vital insights into the solution's effectiveness from those directly impacted. This feedback can be sourced from a diverse array of stakeholders, including customers, employees, and other key parties. It is typically gathered through methods such as surveys, direct interviews, and the analysis of performance data.

Creating effective feedback loop involves gathering, analyzing, and acting upon feedback efficiently. For instance, an educational institution that has moved to digital classrooms might collect feedback from students and teachers about their online learning experience. If feedback highlights issues with the platform's interactive elements, the institution can work with software providers to enhance these features, thus directly responding to the users' needs.

Monitoring progress and conducting follow-ups are critical to ensuring that a solution meets its initial goals and adapts to changing conditions and continuous feedback. This phase requires vigilant oversight, the flexibility to make adjustments, and a robust system for collecting and analyzing feedback. By committing to continuous monitoring and improvement, organizations can sustain the effectiveness of their solutions and address any emerging challenges, thereby maintaining alignment with their long-term strategic objectives.

Summary

Problem-solving and decision-making are complex processes that require a structured, yet flexible approach, blending creative thinking with methodical evaluation. Each of the six steps outlined in this chapter—defining the problem, setting objectives, developing opportunities, selecting the best solution, implementing the solution, and monitoring progress—serves as a vital component in the journey towards effective resolution and successful outcomes.

Starting with a clear definition of the problem sets a solid foundation for the entire process. Setting objectives then provides a clear direction and benchmarks for success, which guide all decision-making efforts. Developing opportunities through brainstorming and other creative techniques opens up a spectrum of possibilities, allowing for a thorough exploration of potential solutions.

The critical task of selecting the best solution involves a thorough analysis of the advantages and disadvantages of each option, considering both the immediate impacts and long-term implications. Once a solution is chosen, the implementation phase is crucial, requiring meticulous planning, resource allocation, and execution to bring the theoretical solution into practical, effective operation.

Monitoring progress and following up are what ensure that the solution remains effective over time. This final step involves continuous evaluation and the flexibility to make adjustments in response to feedback and changing circumstances. It highlights the needs for ongoing vigilance and adaptability in maintaining the efficacy of the solution.

As these principles are applied in various contexts, from personal challenges to professional projects, the key takeaway is the importance of flexibility and adaptability. The dynamic nature of problems requires solutions that are not static but are continually evolving. Successfully navigating this landscape means being open to change and ready to refine your strategies as situations develop.

This approach solves problems, drives innovation, and enhances efficiency, leading to sustained success in any endeavor. As you move forward, remember that the ability to adapt and adjust your approach is crucial. By embracing these principles, you are well-equipped to tackle complex challenges and achieve significant accomplishments in both your personal and professional life.

Chapter Seven

Finance for Non-Finance Professionals

E ffective financial management is crucial for the success of any entity, from established industry giants to growing startups. Central to this management are budgeting and forecasting—key tools that drive long-term strategic planning, decision-making, and resource allocation. These processes do more than computation; they build a financial framework that aligns with an organization's strategic objectives, thereby promoting stability and enabling growth.

Budgeting is a strategic undertaking that involves the detailed planning and allocation of financial resources over a specific period. This essential process is fundamental for setting financial goals, forecasting future revenues and expenses, and ensuring the equitable distribution of resources across various departments and initiatives.

Organizations must realize that employees are far more than mere costs to be minimized—they are invaluable assets, fundamental to driving growth and sparking innovation. Shifting to this mindset is crucial to avoid the trap of shortsighted decisions, like excessive cost-cutting, which often leads to harmful staff reductions aimed at short-term profit gains or quick fixes to financial problems. When employees are seen as core assets, organizations are more likely to invest in their growth and development, resulting in higher productivity, greater innovation, and, ultimately, stronger financial stability and long-term success.

For non-finance professionals to effectively grasp and engage with the financial aspects of their roles, it is crucial that they first acquaint themselves with key financial and accounting principles, including:

Account Payable (AP): This represents the amounts owed by a company for goods purchased on credit, which must be repaid within a short period. It is classified as a liability and falls under the category of 'current liabilities,' a topic that will be elaborated on later in this chapter. Accounts Payable are classified as short-term debt obligations that need to be settled promptly to avoid default.

Account Receivable (AR): This represents the payments or proceeds that a company expects to receive from customers who have purchased its goods or services on credit. The credit period is typically short, ranging from a few days to several months, or, in some cases, up to a year. It is important to monitor Accounts Receivable for potential bad debts, which can include a percentage of sales that may become uncollectible, aging of receivables, and write-offs.

Fiscal Year/Financial Year: A twelve-month period used for accounting and financial reporting purposes, which may or may not align with the calendar year. The specific dates of a fiscal year can vary depending on the sector, company, or country. For instance, academic institutions, government entities, and private businesses may each define their fiscal year differently.

Financial Accounting: Is the branch of accounting that focuses on the preparation of financial statements, which are used by external stakeholders such as investors, creditors, regulators, and the general public to evaluate an organization's financial performance and position. These statements are prepared according to standardized guidelines, such as Generally Accepted Accounting Principles (GAAP) or International Financial Reporting Standards (IFRS), ensuring consistency and comparability across different organizations. The primary objective of financial accounting is to provide a clear and accurate financial overview of a company over a specific period, typically through the income statement, balance sheet, and statement cash flows.

Managerial Accounting: Also known as management accounting, is the process of identifying, measuring, analyzing, and interpreting financial information to help managers make informed decisions within an organization. Unlike financial accounting, managerial accounting is primarily for internal use and is not bound by any standardized reporting rules. This type of accounting focuses on detailed reports and analyses that assist in planning, controlling, and decision-making processes. Managerial accounting provides insights into various aspects of business operations, such as cost behavior, budgeting, performance evaluation, and profitability analysis, enabling managers to optimize resource allocation and improve operational efficiency.

This chapter also aims to explain the principles of financial management for non-finance professionals through various fundamental topics. Through practical examples and detailed explanations, we will explore how non-finance professionals can

177

effectively engage in financial discussions and contribute to their organization's fiscal health and sustainability.

Financial Statements

Financial statements are the backbone of financial accounting, providing a comprehensive view of a company's financial health and performance. Among the various financial documents prepared by businesses, three main standard statements stand out: the Income Statement (commonly known as the Profit & Loss or P&L Statement), the Balance Sheet (also referred to as the Statement of Financial Position), and the Statement of Cash Flows. These statements are critical tools for internal management and serve as key resources for external stakeholders, including investors, creditors, regulators, and analysts, who rely on them to make informed decisions.

In this section, we will cover each of these financial statements in greater detail, examining their structure, purpose, and the key benefits they offer. By the end of this discussion, readers will have a thorough understanding of how these financial statements work together to provide a complete picture of a company's financial health, enabling better decision-making and strategic planning.

Income Statement

Income statement (Figure 23), often referred to as the Profit & Loss (P&L) Statement, is one of the most critical financial documents used to evaluate a company's financial performance over a specific period. It provides a detailed summary of all revenues generated and expenses incurred during that period, ultimately revealing the company's net profit or loss. The primary purpose of the income statement is to provide stakeholders with a clear picture of the company's operational effectiveness and profitability, helping them assess whether the business is generating sufficient income to cover its costs and contribute to growth.

The income statement is meticulously organized to provide a clear view of the company's financial performance, categorized into four main sections:

1. **Revenues**

This section captures the total earnings from the company's primary business operations, which includes gross sales and other revenue streams such as interest and investments.

2. **Expenses**
   - **Cost of Goods Sold (COGS):** This includes direct costs associated with producing or acquiring the goods the company sells, such as materials, labor, and manufacturing overhead. Gross profit is determined by subtracting COGS from revenue.

   - **Operating Expenses:** Covers all the necessary costs for operating the business that are not directly linked to production, including salaries, rent, utilities, marketing, and administrative expenses. Operating income is derived by subtracting these expenses from the gross profit, reflecting the core business profitability.

3. **Below-the-Line Items**

Non-operating items which consist of revenues and expenses not directly related to primary business operations, such as gains or losses from asset sales and interest. Additionally, this category includes income from discontinued operations, the effects of accounting changes, and extraordinary items, providing a complete view of all factors influencing profitability beyond regular operations.

4. Net Income

This represents the final profit or loss calculated after all revenues, expenses, and below-the-line items have been accounted for. This figure is essential for assessing the company's overall financial health and is utilized to calculate key metrics like Earnings Per Share (EPS).

The income statement is crucial for both internal and external stakeholders. For internal management, it acts as a pivotal tool for monitoring operational efficiency, controlling costs, and enhancing profitability. Through systematic analysis of revenue and expense trends, management can make informed decisions regarding pricing strategies, cost management, and resource distribution.

For external stakeholders such as investors, creditors, and analysts, the income statement offers vital insights into the company's financial health and its potential for future success. Investors might use the statement to evaluate the company's profitability and growth potential, aiding them in decisions related to buying, holding, or selling shares. Creditors rely on it to assess the company's capacity to repay debts, while analysts might benchmark it against industry standards to evaluate competitive positioning.

[Company Name]	Income Statement	
	For the Years Ending [Dec 31, 2024 and Dec 31, 2023]	
Revenue	**2024**	**2023**
Sales revenue	220,000	190,000
(Less sales returns and allowances)		
Service revenue	70,000	62,000
Interest revenue		
Other revenue		
Total Revenues	**290,000**	**252,000**
Expenses		
Advertising	1,500	1,500
Bad debt		
Commissions		
Cost of goods sold	97,500	94,500
Depreciation		
Employee benefits		
Furniture and equipment		12,000
Insurance		
Interest expense	6,300	7,800
Maintenance and repairs		
Office supplies		
Payroll taxes		
Rent		
Research and development		
Salaries and wages	82,500	82,500
Software		
Travel		
Utilities		
Web hosting and domains		
Other	26,190	
Total Expenses	**213,990**	**198,300**
Net Income Before Taxes	76,010	53,700
Income tax expense	22,404	14,880
Income from Continuing Operations	**53,606**	**38,820**
Below-the-Line Items		
Income from discontinued operations		
Effect of accounting changes		
Extraordinary items		
Net Income	**53,606**	**38,820**

Figure 23. Income Statement

To illustrate the practical application of the income statement, consider a company that signs a $500,000 contract in December, receiving a $100,000 advance. If the project is scheduled to start in January of the following year, the $100,000 should not appear in

December's income statement. According to the accrual accounting principle, revenue is recognized when earned, not when received. Recording the advance as December revenue would misrepresent the company's financial performance for that period, as the revenue is unearned until the project commences.

Similarly, expenses related to the project should only be recognized once incurred, ensuring the income statement accurately reflects operational profitability for the specific period.

For instance, if a company reports a high net income for a quarter, it may initially attract investors. However, if this profitability stems from one-off events like asset sales, rather than regular operations, it might mislead stakeholders about the company's ongoing financial health. A detailed analysis of the income statement components is essential beyond just the final figures.

In the hospitality sector, one company noticed declining profits despite steady revenues. A thorough analysis of its income statement revealed that increasing operational costs, particularly for food and labor, were diminishing profit margins. This led to strategic cost reviews and implementations of measures such as renegotiating supplier contracts and optimizing labor allocations, which subsequently improved profitability.

In conclusion, the income statement is an essential financial tool that provides detailed insights into revenues and expenses, enabling stakeholders to determine whether a company is operating profitably. This information is vital for making informed business decisions, evaluating financial health, and planning strategic initiatives for future growth.

Balance Sheet

The balance sheet (also referred to as the Statement of Financial Position) is a fundamental financial statement that provides a snapshot of a company's financial position at a specific point in time (Figure 24). Unlike the income statement, which reflects financial performance over a period, the balance sheet captures the company's economic resources (assets) and obligations (liabilities) on a particular date. This snapshot is vital for stakeholders like investors, creditors, and management, enabling them to assess the company's financial health and stability.

The balance sheet conforms to the essential accounting formula: **Assets = Liabilities + Equity**. This equation outlines the relationship between the company's assets—its owned resources—and its liabilities—its financial obligations. The resultant figure, owners' equity, signifies the net value or net worth of the company. From the sheet, it is observable that assets are categorized into current (short-term) assets, fixed (long-term) assets, and other assets, encompassing items like cash, accounts receivable, and property. Liabilities, divided into current and long-term, include accounts payable and loans.

The equity section comprises components such as common stock, retained earnings, and additional paid-in capital, showcasing the residual interest in the company's assets after accounting for all liabilities. This structured representation provides stakeholders with a clear view of the company's financial health and stability.

[Company Name]	Balance Sheet	
	Date: 12/31/2024	
Assets	**2020**	**2019**
Current Assets		
Cash	11,874	
Accounts receivable		
Inventory		
Prepaid expenses		
Short-term investments		
Total current assets $	11,874 $	-
Fixed (Long-Term) Assets		
Long-term investments	1,208	
Property, plant, and equipment	15,340	
(Less accumulated depreciation)	(2,200)	
Intangible assets		
Total fixed assets $	14,348 $	-
Other Assets		
Deferred income tax		
Other		
Total Other Assets $	- $	-
Total Assets	**$ 26,222** **$**	**-**
Liabilities and Owner's Equity		
Current Liabilities		
Accounts payable	8,060	
Short-term loans		
Income taxes payable	3,145	
Accrued salaries and wages		
Unearned revenue		
Current portion of long-term debt		
Total current liabilities $	11,205 $	-
Long-Term Liabilities		
Long-term debt	3,450	
Deferred income tax		
Other		
Total long-term liabilities $	3,450 $	-
Owner's Equity		
Owner's investment	7,178	
Retained earnings	4,389	
Other		
Total owner's equity $	11,567 $	-
Total Liabilities and Owner's Equity	**$ 26,222** **$**	**-**

Figure 24. Balance Sheet

The balance sheet enables decision-makers to gauge the company's financial position by analyzing the balance between its assets, liabilities, and equity. For instance, a company with a substantial asset base and manageable liabilities may be considered financially stable, whereas one with high liabilities relative to assets could be viewed as at risk.

To illustrate the balance sheet's practical application, consider the $100,000 advance payment from a previously mentioned example. A company signed a $500,000 contract in December, with the project slated to start in January. Since the project has not commenced, the $100,000 should not appear as revenue on the income statement. Instead, it is recorded on the balance sheet under liabilities as Unearned Revenue or Accounts Payable. This entry reflects the company's commitment to deliver service or product in the future, consistent with the principle that revenues and expenses should be recognized when they are actually earned or incurred.

In summary, the balance sheet is a crucial tool for understanding a company's financial standing. By clearly outlining the company's assets, liabilities, and equity, it equips stakeholders with the information necessary to make educated assessments about the company's financial strength, liquidity, and overall stability.

Statement of Cash Flows

The statement of cash flows is a vital financial document that provides detailed information about a company's cash inflows and outflows over a specific period. Unlike the income statement, which shows profitability, and the balance sheet, which provides a snapshot of financial position, the statement of cash flows focuses exclusively on the movement of cash within the business. This statement is crucial because it helps stakeholders understand how well the company manages its cash, ensuring it has enough liquidity to meet its obligations and invest in growth.

The statement of cash flows, as illustrated in the example of Figure 25, is organized into three primary sections that delineate the company's cash management strategies and outcomes:

Operating Activities: This section presents the cash inflows and outflows stemming from the company's core business activities. It encompasses cash receipts from the sales of goods and services, cash payments made to suppliers and employees, and other expenditures related to the daily operations. The net cash flow from operating activities, totaling $568,450, serves as a vital gauge of the company's capability to generate enough cash to sustain and expand its operations.

Investing Activities: Detailing the cash movements associated with the purchase and sale of long-term assets and investments, this section of the statement of cash flows provides a snapshot of how the company is investing in its future growth and sustainability. Cash outflows here might involve the acquisition of new equipment or properties, totaling a net outflow of $45,300, while inflows could arise from the sale of assets or earnings from investments.

Financing Activities: Reflecting the financial strategies of the company, this section tracks cash flows related to financing activities such as issuing or repaying debt, distributing dividends, and the trading of company stock. Notable cash inflows may originate from new equity or debt instruments, while outflows are generally associated with dividend payments or debt payments, summing up to a net outflow of $130,500. This section is crucial for understanding how the company structures its finances to support operations and facilitate growth, highlighting its capital management approach.

[Company Name] Statement of Cash Flows	
For the Year Ending	12/31/2024
Cash at Beginning of Year	31,400
Operations	
Cash receipts from	
Customers	1,386,400
Other Operations	
Cash paid for	
Inventory purchases	(396,000)
General operating and administrative expenses	(168,000)
Wage expenses	(184,500)
Interest	(20,250)
Income taxes	(49,200)
Net Cash Flow from Operations	**568,450**
Investing Activities	
Cash receipts from	
Sale of property and equipment	67,200
Collection of principal on loans	
Sale of investment securities	
Cash paid for	
Purchase of property and equipment	(112,500)
Making loans to other entities	
Purchase of investment securities	
Net Cash Flow from Investing Activities	**(45,300)**
Financing Activities	
Cash receipts from	
Issuance of stock	
Borrowing	
Cash paid for	
Repurchase of stock (treasury stock)	
Repayment of loans	(51,000)
Dividends	(79,500)
Net Cash Flow from Financing Activities	**(130,500)**
Net Increase in Cash	**392,650**
Cash at End of Year	424,050

Figure 25. Statement of Cash Flows

Each of these sections contributes to the overall financial narrative of the company, depicting how it manages cash to support its operations, invest in its future, and structure its financing. The net increase in cash for the period, amounting to $392,650, indicates the company's effective cash management practices during the fiscal period.

The statement of cash flows is a vital tool for both internal management and external stakeholders, offering crucial insights into a company's cash management. It enables internal management to ensure sufficient liquidity is maintained to meet short-term obligations and to fund long-term projects. By analyzing trends in cash flow, management can make informed decisions about budgeting, investment, and financing strategies.

For external stakeholders like creditors and investors, the statement of cash flows provides a transparent view of the company's ability to generate cash. Creditors use this statement to determine the company's capacity to repay loans, carefully examining it before extending credit to minimize the risk of default.

Consider a scenario where a company seeks a loan for a new project. A lender would review the company's cash flow statement, paying close attention to the cash generated from operations. A consistent positive cash flow from operations indicates a strong internal cash generation, instilling confidence in the lender about the company's repayment abilities.

Conversely, if a company exhibits negative cash flow from operations or relies heavily on external financing, a lender might perceive higher risk. This might lead to demands for higher interest rates or additional guarantees, or the lender might even refuse the loan application.

For instance, a rapidly expanding startup, despite increasing sales, may find that its operating cash flow remains negative due to significant expenditures on research, marketing, and personnel. Such insights can prompt management to seek additional funding sources or manage cash outflows more carefully to sustain growth.

During economic downturns, a manufacturing company might face sales declines leading to cash flow challenges. By reviewing the cash flow statement, which might show inadequate operating cash to cover fixed expenses, the company can take strategic actions such as cost reduction or enhancing receivables collection to navigate through tough times.

In essence, the statement of cash flows is crucial for depicting a detailed account of a company's cash inflows and outflows. It enables stakeholders, particularly creditors, to gauge the company's liquidity, financial stability, and operational efficiency. Understanding and analyzing these flows is essential for making informed financial decisions and ensuring the company's ongoing viability.

Moreover, to effectively manage their financial health, companies typically produce cash flow statements on a quarterly or monthly basis. This practice provides a continuous overview of cash movements, allowing companies to observe and react to seasonal patterns, sudden changes in market conditions, or any irregularities that occur throughout the fiscal year. Frequent cash flow analysis is vital for maintaining a clear picture of liquidity and operational efficiency, and it enables proactive financial management. These regular updates also allow stakeholders to track the company's progress against its financial objectives, facilitating more strategic planning and decision-making.

The Enron scandal is a critical study in the misuse of financial statements. It showcases how Enron misrepresented its financial health by fabricating earnings and hiding debt, leading to one of the most infamous corporate collapses in history. This case underscores the importance of ethical financial reporting and the severe consequences of deceptive practices. It highlights the need for transparency and integrity in financial reporting and has had lasting impacts on regulatory practices, including the introduction of the Sarbanes-Oxley Act to enhance corporate accountability.

While financial statements are indispensable tools for assessing an organization's financial health, they come with limitations. They are historical and may not reflect current or imminent conditions. Valuations of certain items may involve subjectivity, which may not accurately depict true market values.

Additionally, financial statements do not include non-financial factors like market dynamics or regulatory changes, which can significantly affect a company's performance. Recognizing these limitations is crucial when using financial statements for decision-making, and they should be supplemented with other analytical tools and market insights to provide a comprehensive view of a company's status.

Budgeting Planning and Forecasting

Budgeting planning and forecasting are foundational components of financial management that steer an organization's strategic decision-making and resource allocation. These processes enable businesses to set financial goals, predict future performance, and respond effectively to market dynamics.

A robust budget acts as a financial blueprint, guiding daily operations and enabling organizations to maintain fiscal discipline, monitor performance, and adapt strategies as necessary. Furthermore, budgeting is pivotal for aligning financial resources with organizational objectives, anticipating future financial requirements, and managing cash flows to avert potential fiscal deficits.

Budget planning is essential for various reasons:

Understanding the current financial position: Budgets help organizations understand where they stand financially and what resources are available for future investments or expenditures.

Aligning financial plans with goals: A well-crafted budget ensures that resources are distributed in line with the company's strategic objectives.

Crisis prevention: A budget highlights potential financial risks, allowing management to adjust before a crisis occurs. This proactive approach ensures financial stability over time.

Coordination and communication: A budget serves as a communication tool between departments, ensuring that everyone works toward the same financial goals.

Scenario planning: Budgets allow companies to simulate different scenarios and prepare for potential challenges.

Organizations can use different types of budgets depending on their needs:

Operational Budget: Outlines the expected income and expenses related to the day-to-day operations of the organization. It is typically used to ensure that the company can cover its operating costs and achieve profitability.

Capital Budget: Used for planning and managing significant investments in long-term assets, such as new machinery, buildings, or technology systems. It helps organizations evaluate the financial viability of these investments.

Cash Flow Budget: Focuses on forecasting the cash inflows and outflows over a specific period. It is essential for ensuring that the company has sufficient liquidity to meet its obligations.

Master Budget: A comprehensive financial plan that includes all the smaller, individual budgets within an organization. It provides an overview of the organization's financial position and is used for overall strategic planning.

By ensuring efficient resource allocation, aligning operations with long-term objectives, and providing insights into potential financial outcomes, organizations can remain agile, mitigate risks, and achieve sustainable growth.

Budgeting Approaches

Budgeting within organizations can typically be approached in two fundamental ways, each distinct in its application and suited to different management styles and organizational structures:

Top-Down Approach: In this strategy, senior management develops the budget based on the organization's overall strategic goals, allocating funds across various departments to ensure alignment with these objectives. While this approach promotes uniformity across the organization and ensures all units strive towards common goals, it may not fully leverage the detailed insights that lower-level managers have regarding day-to-day operations and specific departmental needs.

Bottom-Up Approach: In contrast, the bottom-up approach initiates at the departmental level, where budgets are formulated based on detailed operational needs and then escalated to senior management for approval. This method enhances accuracy and practicality in the budgeting process by accounting for the specific requirements and constraints of each department. However, it might also encourage budget slack, where managers could inflate their financial requests to secure surplus resources, which could lead to inefficiencies.

To capitalize on the advantages of both foundational approaches, many organizations adopt a hybrid strategy. This model merges the strategic oversight of the top-down approach with the operational precision of the bottom-up method, providing an effective blend that improves the balance between strategic consistency and responsiveness to actual operational needs.

For instance, a company might establish broad financial goals at the corporate level while allowing individual departments the flexibility to tailor their budgets based on immediate operational needs and market conditions. This integrated approach ensures that departments are aligned with the company's strategic objectives and empowers them to manage resources efficiently, enhancing accountability and adaptability across the organization.

By adopting this sophisticated approach to budgeting, organizations effectively bridge the gap between high-level strategic planning and ground-level operational needs, accommodating both the vision of management and the practical realities faced by individual departments.

Zero-Based Budgeting (ZBB)

It is important to also consider Zero-Based Budgeting, a distinct budgeting method that requires all expenses to be justified for each new period, starting from a "zero base." Budgets are constructed based on the needs of the upcoming period, regardless of previous budget allocations. While ZBB can be time-intensive, it tends to favor areas that directly generate revenue or production, as their contributions are more easily justified. On the other hand, departments like client services and research and development may find it challenging to justify their budgets under this approach, as their value is often less directly measurable.

The Role of Forecasting in Budgeting

Forecasting, while intimately linked to budgeting, extends its reach by predicting future financial outcomes based on historical data, market trends, and other external factors. This proactive process equips organizations to foresee potential challenges and capitalize on emerging opportunities.

Conversely, sales forecasting is a cornerstone of the budgeting process. It entails the projection of future sales volumes and revenues, which critically inform the development of a comprehensive budget. The precision of sales forecasting is vital because it impacts all related budget components, including production, staffing, and marketing strategies.

In companies specializing in consumer electronics, such as smartphones and tablets, the budgeting process starts with a comprehensive sales forecast. This forecast relies on historical sales data, market analysis, and emerging trends in consumer technology to estimate future sales volumes and revenue.

To ensure efficiency, these companies align departmental budgets closely with their strategic objectives. This alignment optimizes resource allocation and streamlines operational planning. By employing this integrated approach, they effectively manage production, meet market demand, and drive profitability. Such strategic alignment enhances daily operations and strengthens the company's long-term competitiveness in a dynamic market.

In industries like airlines or hospitality, sales forecasts are based on metrics like passenger numbers or room occupancy rates. Misalignments in sales forecasting can lead to overproduction or stock shortages, each carrying significant financial consequences. For example, a fashion retail company faced challenges from seasonal trends and fluctuating consumer preferences but improved

195

its forecasting accuracy by employing a model that incorporated historical sales data and market trends.

For forecasting purposes, companies also need to consider historical data, governmental and international policies, economic conditions, technological advancements, consumer needs, competition intensity, strategic plans, seasonal cycles, and unforeseen events.

A notable case involved an automotive manufacturer that launched a new model based on overly optimistic sales forecasts, only to face substantial financial losses due to unsold inventory surpluses. This situation underscores the importance of grounding sales forecasting in realistic assumptions and accurate data to prevent costly miscalculations.

This robust approach to budgeting and forecasting is fundamental for companies navigating the complexities of a dynamic business environment, ensuring they remain resilient and responsive to market demands.

When transactions involve multiple currencies, fluctuations in exchange rates can create variances. To mitigate this risk and achieve more stable financial outcomes, companies use various financial instruments that secure predictable exchange rates and protect against potential losses from currency volatility. These measures help businesses preserve budget accuracy and financial stability despite the uncertainties of the global market.

Budgetary Slack/Padding: This term describes the practice of intentionally underestimating revenues or overestimating costs in a budget. This approach is often used to create a cushion, making it easier to exceed budget expectations and, as a result, make performance appear more favorable. Essentially, it is a strategy where individuals build in extra room to manage uncertainty or unexpected expenses. For instance, in the stock market, companies might use budgetary slack to ensure they meet or exceed investor expectations. Similarly, when planning a summer vacation, one might overestimate costs to ensure a comfortable financial buffer.

Master Budget Components

A master budget is a comprehensive financial planning document that consolidates various specific budgets related to different aspects of a company's operations (refer to Figure 26).

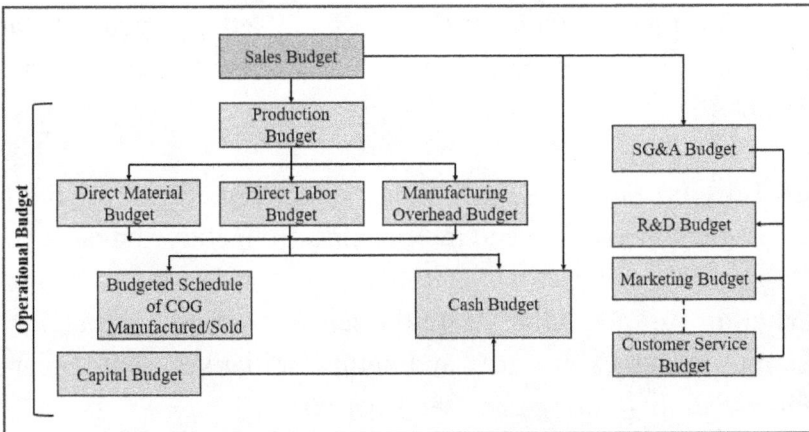

Figure 26. Illustration of a Master Budget Components

This budget typically includes several critical components:

Sales Budget: Estimates expected sales revenue based on historical data and market trends.

Production Budget: Specifies the volume of production needed to meet anticipated sales, ensuring adequate supply.

Direct Materials, Direct Labor, and Manufacturing Overhead Budgets: These budgets calculate the direct costs associated with producing goods or services.

Cash Budget: Forecasts cash inflows and outflows, crucial for maintaining sufficient liquidity.

Capital Budget: Details planned capital expenditures, such as investments in new equipment or facility expansions, to support growth.

SG&A Budget: Covers the necessary selling, general, and administrative expenses essential for day-to-day business operations.

R&D Budget: Funds research and development efforts, crucial for technological innovation and maintaining competitive advantage.

Marketing Budget: Aligns with the sales projections, strategically directing resources towards marketing initiatives that enhance product visibility during peak sales periods.

Customer Service Budget: Supports anticipated increases in sales with enhanced customer service capabilities, budgeting for additional personnel and resources to improve customer satisfaction.

Budgeted Financial Statements: Includes pro forma income statements, balance sheets, and statement of cash flows, providing a projected financial outlook at the end of the budget period.

For example, a medium-sized manufacturing company leverages the master budget to align its production, procurement, and financial strategies. With an expected increase in demand projected at 10%, the company enhances its production capabilities reflected in an expanded production budget and capital investments in new machinery. The cash budget is meticulously planned to ensure there are adequate funds to finance these expansions without excessive borrowing.

This explores the complexities of budgeting planning and forecasting with detailed explanations and practical examples. By integrating these components effectively, businesses ensure financial stability and accurate forecasting, crucial for successful corporate management.

Understanding Budget Variance

Budget variance refers to the deviation between actual financial outcomes and the projections set in the budget. Regular monitoring and justification of significant variances are essential, especially during budget review meetings, to ensure that an organization adheres to its financial objectives.

For instance, XYZ Manufacturing frequently encountered issues with budget variances due to forecasting errors. To mitigate this, the company integrated rolling forecasts and scenario planning into its strategy, enabling continuous updates to its budget. This adjustment significantly minimized variances and enhanced the company's overall financial performance, with major discrepancies being thoroughly analyzed and justified in review sessions.

Enterprise Resource Planning (ERP) Systems

ERP systems play a pivotal role in modern budgeting and forecasting processes by integrating various business functions into a comprehensive platform for financial planning. These systems allow organizations to conduct sensitivity analyses, consolidate individual unit budgets into a comprehensive master budget, and produce detailed financial reports.

Advancements in technology, including cloud-based ERP systems and Artificial Intelligence (AI) algorithms, have further refined these processes. For instance, a retail company utilized an AI-driven forecasting tool that leveraged historical sales data, weather patterns, and social media trends to anticipate future sales, enabling real-time inventory adjustments.

In this section, we have discussed the essentials of budgeting planning and forecasting. We examined various budgeting techniques, underscored the significance of precise sales forecasting, and discussed the integral role of ERP systems in refining the budgeting process. Additionally, we dissected the elements of a master budget and their collective function in formulating a thorough financial strategy for an organization. Through practical illustrations and comprehensive explanations, we have emphasized the crucial role of these processes in maintaining accurate budget forecasts and achieving financial stability, ensuring any significant variances are promptly addressed and justified.

Capital Budgeting

Capital budgeting is a pivotal financial process crucial for planning and evaluating substantial investments in long-term assets that are essential for a company's growth, sustainability, and profitability. Such assets, including new equipment, buildings, or technology, are critical to a company's operations and are expected to yield returns over an extended period.

The main objective of capital budgeting is to identify and allocate resources to projects that will maximize the company's profitability and enhance shareholder value. This process demands a rigorous analysis of potential returns and associated risks due to the significant financial commitments and the long-term implications of these investments.

Distinguishing Between CAPEX and OPEX

It is vital to differentiate between capital expenditures (CAPEX) and operating expenses (OPEX) in capital budgeting:

- **Capital Expenditures (CAPEX):** These are investments in major physical assets or services expected to be useful for more than one year, such as machinery, buildings, or technology systems. These assets are capitalized on the balance sheet and depreciated over their useful lives.

- **Operating Expenses (OPEX):** These are daily operational costs like utilities, salaries, and rent. OPEX is expensed fully in the period they are incurred and reported on the income statement.

Understanding the distinction is critical since capital budgeting focuses on long-term investments, known as CAPEX, which influence the company's financial performance over several years.

Examples of capital budgeting decisions can include the following:

- **Starting a New Business:** Requires significant CAPEX in infrastructure, technology, and initial human resources setup.

- **Investment in a New Production Plant:** Expanding production capacity involves substantial long-term capital expenditure.

- **Implementing an ERP System:** Involves significant CAPEX on software and infrastructure.

- **Purchasing Vehicles or Office Furniture:** These are long-term assets whose costs are capitalized.

Capital Budgeting Risks

Capital budgeting decisions carry inherent risks due to their long-term nature and significant financial commitment. Common risks include:

- **Market Risk**: Changes in the market can affect the expected returns from an investment.

- **Financial Risk**: Using debt to fund investments can increase financial leverage and affect profitability.

- **Operational Risk**: Successful implementation is crucial, and failures can lead to project delays or cost overruns.

- **Regulatory Risk**: Legal changes can affect the feasibility or profitability of a project.

Given these risks, companies must conduct a thorough analysis before making capital budgeting decisions. For instance, before deciding whether to lease or purchase an office building, a company would analyze both options using various capital budgeting models to determine the most cost-effective and strategically sound choice.

Capital Investment Analysis Methods

Capital investment analysis methods play a pivotal role in assessing the potential returns and risks of long-term investments within the framework of capital budgeting. These methods enable businesses to identify projects and investments that enhance overall value. Each method comes with its own set of strengths and limitations, encouraging companies to adopt a combination of approaches for a thorough evaluation of an investment's feasibility and profitability.

To streamline these analyses, businesses frequently leverage advanced software tools and applications, ensuring informed decision-making.

Payback Period
- **Definition:** The amount of time it takes for an investment to generate cash flows sufficient to recover the initial investment cost.

- **Example:** Suppose your company invests $10,000 in a new machine that saves $2,500 annually in labor costs. The payback period would be $10,000 / $2,500 = 4 years.
- **Disadvantage:** Does not account for the value of money over time or cash flows beyond the payback period.

Accounting Rate of Return (ARR)

- **Definition:** Also known as Average Rate of Return, calculates the average annual profit from an investment relative to the average investment cost, expressed as a percentage. This measure provides an overview of the expected profitability of an investment over its useful life.
- **Example:** If an investment costs $50,000 and is expected to generate an average annual profit of $7,000, the ARR would be ($7,000 / $50,000) * 100 = 14%.
- **Disadvantage:** Ignores the time value of money. Additionally, it can be distorted by non-cash items such as depreciation, which, though not involving actual cash outflow, reduces reported annual profits.

Net Present Value (NPV)

- **Definition:** The sum of the present values of incoming and outgoing cash flows over a period of time. A positive NPV indicates that the returns from an investment exceed the discount rate applied in the calculations, signifying that the investment is likely to be profitable.
- **Example:** An investment of $100,000 that is expected to return $30,000 annually over 5 years with a discount rate of 8% would have an NPV of about $19,781. This means the investment would earn more than the cost of capital.

- **Disadvantage:** Requires an accurate discount rate to be effective, which can be difficult to estimate.

Internal Rate of Return (IRR)

- **Definition:** The discount rate that makes the NPV of all cash flows from a particular project equal to zero. It represents the annual growth rate an investment is expected to generate.
- **Example:** If an investment requires an initial outlay of $100,000 and is expected to generate returns of $40,000 annually for the next three years, the IRR would be approximately 9.70%.
- **Disadvantage:** Can give misleading results with non-conventional cash flows which occur when there are additional negative cash flows after the initial investment period. This can happen in cases like reinvestment requirements or large operational expenses occurring after the start of an investment. Additionally, it assumes that the interim cash flows generated by the project are reinvested at a rate of return equal to the IRR itself.

Return on Investment (ROI)

- **Definition:** A performance measure used to evaluate the efficiency of an investment, calculated by dividing the net profit by the cost of the investment.
- **Example:** If you spend $20,000 on marketing and it leads to additional sales of $50,000 with a net profit (after all expenses) of $10,000, the ROI would be ($10,000 / $20,000) * 100 = 50%.
- **Disadvantage:** Does not take into account the duration of the investment, which can lead to inaccurate analyses when

comparing investments that require different time periods to generate returns.

Combining Methods for Comprehensive Analysis

Companies often employ more than one capital budgeting method to gain a well-rounded understanding of an investment's potential financial outcomes. Using multiple methods compensates for the individual shortcomings of each technique and allows decision-makers to assess different aspects of the investment's financial viability.

For instance, while NPV provides a sense of an investment's value creation, IRR offers insight into its profitability rate, and the payback period indicates liquidity risk. This multifaceted approach ensures that strategic financial decisions are made with a thorough consideration of both potential returns and associated risks.

The Capital Budgeting Process

The capital budgeting process generally follows these steps:

- **Develop Strategies**: Align potential investments with the company's strategic objectives.

- **Planning**: Thoroughly evaluate potential projects to assess their expected returns and risks.

- **Act**: Implement the selected investment and allocate the necessary resources.

- **Control**: Monitor the investment's performance to ensure it meets the expected outcomes and make necessary adjustments.

This section has covered the essentials of capital budgeting, providing insights into the complexities of managing large-scale investments and their critical role in fostering corporate growth and profitability. By understanding and applying the principles discussed, companies and individuals can make informed decisions that optimize their financial resources and sustain long-term growth.

Depreciation

Depreciation is the systematic allocation of the cost of a long-term asset over the periods benefiting from its use, accounting for the asset's gradual decline in value due to factors like wear and tear, and obsolescence.

Causes of Depreciation:

Depreciation occurs as assets lose value, driven by specific underlying causes. Key contributors to depreciation include:

- **Physical Deterioration**: Assets such as vehicles, machinery, and buildings naturally degrade over time, diminishing their functionality and value. For instance, a delivery truck depreciates with increased mileage and wear, requiring more frequent maintenance.

- **Obsolescence**: Technological advancements and shifts in market demands can render assets outdated even before their physical deterioration. For example, a rapid pace of innovation in technology sectors can make earlier versions of computers and software obsolete, diminishing their operational relevance.

Depreciation is a fundamental component in accounting and financial management, as it allows for a better understanding of the cost of utilizing assets over their lifespan. This facilitates informed financial decision-making and precise financial planning.

Non-depreciable Assets

Land is generally classified as a non-depreciable asset in accounting because it does not deteriorate with time or use. Unlike other tangible assets, land does not lose its value through physical wear and tear or technological obsolescence. This enduring nature sets land apart in financial reporting and asset management.

However, there are exceptions to this general rule when the land contains depletable resources. If land has inherent natural resources like minerals, oil, or gas, it can undergo depreciation through a process known as depletion. Depletion is the allocation of the cost of natural resources over the period they are extracted and sold. This specific type of depreciation recognizes the consumption of the land's economic value as the resources are gradually removed.

When purchasing land that includes a building or other structures, accounting practices require that the purchase price be allocated between the land and the building based on their respective market values. This distinction is crucial because, while the land remains non-depreciable, the building on it is subject to depreciation. The building's depreciation is calculated based on its useful life, reflecting the reduction in value due to factors such as physical deterioration and obsolescence. This separation ensures accurate financial reporting and tax calculation, allowing businesses to claim depreciation expenses for the building while preserving the land's value intact on the balance sheet.

By understanding the details of land valuation and the depreciation of associated assets, businesses can ensure compliance with accounting standards and make informed decisions about property investment and management. This knowledge is especially important in industries where real estate plays a critical role, such as construction, manufacturing, and real estate development.

Methods of Calculating Depreciation

Depreciation is an accounting method used to allocate the cost of a tangible or physical asset over its useful life. The concept reflects the decrease in value of an asset over time due to factors like wear and tear, obsolescence, or age. It's an essential practice in accounting because it helps companies spread the cost of an asset over the period it is used to generate revenue, thus matching revenues with expenses in accordance with the matching principle in accounting.

The choice of depreciation method can significantly affect a company's financial statements and tax obligations. Various methods offer different rates and patterns of expense recognition over the asset's operational life, impacting net income, cash flows, and asset valuation on the balance sheet. Selecting the appropriate depreciation method is crucial for accurate financial representation and can serve strategic purposes, influencing financial indicators such as earnings before interest, taxes, depreciation, and amortization (EBITDA), net income, and the company's tax liability.

Different methods of depreciation are used depending on the nature of the asset and the financial goals of the company. Some methods might be better suited for assets that quickly lose value or become outdated, while others might be ideal for assets that have a longer, more consistent useful life. The decision involves considering how the asset's value diminishes over time.

Two key methods predominantly used in this calculation are the Straight-Line Depreciation and the Double Declining Balance Method (Figure 27).

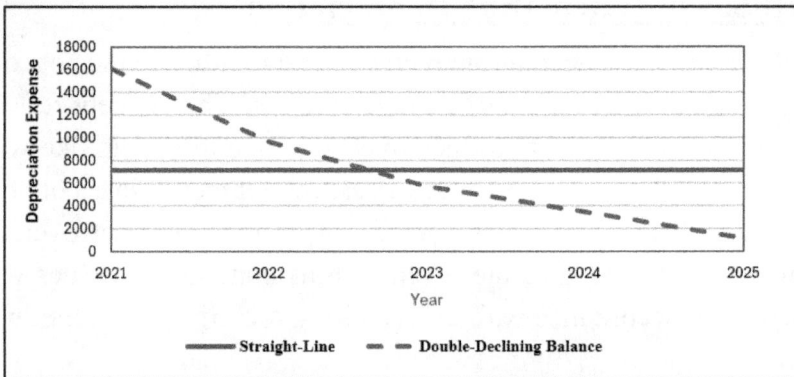

Figure 27. Two of the Depreciation Methods

Each method offers a different approach based on the asset's usage, value retention, and business financial strategy, impacting how costs are allocated during the asset's productive life. These methodologies not only help in accurate financial reporting but also in strategic planning regarding asset management and tax liabilities.

- **Straight-Line Method:** This is the simplest form of calculating depreciation, distributing an equal amount of expense over the asset's useful life. For instance, if a piece of equipment costs $40,000, has a residual value of $4,000, and a useful life of 5 years, the annual depreciation would be $(40,000 - 4,000) / 5 = \$7,200$. Each year, $7,200 is expensed, steadily reducing the asset's book value.

- **Double Declining Balance (DDB) Method:** This accelerated method front-loads depreciation expenses, applying double the straight-line rate to the declining book value each year. Using the previous example, the first year's depreciation would be 40% of $40,000, amounting to $16,000, with the asset's book value and subsequent depreciation amounts reducing each year.

Amortization is similar to depreciation but applies specifically to intangible assets. It allocates the cost of assets such as patents, trademarks, licenses, or software over their expected useful lives. For example, amortizing a $50,000 patent over a 10-year period would result in an annual expense of $5,000. This method ensures that the expense recognition aligns with the benefit derived from the asset over time.

In the United States, the Modified Accelerated Cost Recovery System (MACRS) is utilized specifically for tax depreciation purposes and does not align with Generally Accepted Accounting Principles (GAAP). MACRS allows businesses to accelerate depreciation on their assets, leading to substantial tax benefits in the early years of an asset's life. This method significantly enhances a firm's cash flow by reducing taxable income swiftly, which is advantageous for tax planning but should not be confused with financial reporting methods.

It is important for companies to maintain separate depreciation calculations—one for tax purposes using MACRS and another for financial statements in compliance with GAAP — to accurately reflect the economic value of assets and their financial condition.

Book Value vs. Market Value

- **Book Value:** Calculated as original cost minus accumulated depreciation, reflecting the accounting value of an asset.

- **Market Value:** The potential selling price in the current market, which can diverge significantly from book value.

Depreciation Recapture

Occurs when an asset sells for more than its book value, requiring the excess to be reported as income, such as when equipment sold at $35,000 exceeds its $20,000 book value by $15,000.

Impact on Financial Statements

Depreciation is a non-cash expense that, despite not affecting cash flow directly, plays a significant role in financial management. By lowering taxable income, depreciation reduces a company's tax liabilities, which indirectly increases available cash flow. This increment in cash flow can be strategically used for reinvestment, expansion, or debt servicing.

Effects on Profitability and Asset Valuation

Depreciation impacts financial statements in two primary ways:

- **Profitability**: On the income statement, depreciation is recorded as an expense, which reduces reported earnings or net profit for the period. While it lowers profitability on paper, the expense does not involve any cash outflow, allowing the funds to be used elsewhere in the business.

- **Asset Valuation**: On the balance sheet, accumulated depreciation decreases the book value of the asset. This reduction reflects the decreasing usefulness and economic value of the asset over time, aligning its book value more closely with its current worth or market value.

In summary, depreciation is more than just an accounting principle—it significantly shapes a company's financial reporting, analysis, and strategic decision-making. By systematically allocating the cost of tangible assets over their useful lives, depreciation ensures that financial statements reflect the gradual consumption of assets, which directly influences a company's profitability, tax obligations, and overall financial position.

Furthermore, its effect on key performance indicators like return on assets, net income, and cash flow underscores its importance in financial planning and analysis. A clear understanding of depreciation allows companies to accurately manage capital expenditures, make informed investment decisions, and project future cash needs.

Additionally, by transparently communicating asset values and their ongoing depreciation, businesses can foster trust and credibility with stakeholders such as investors, lenders, and regulatory bodies. Ultimately, proper management and reporting of depreciation contribute to the long-term financial health and sustainability of the organization, reinforcing both its operational efficiency and its alignment with financial goals.

Inventory

Inventory is a critical component for businesses, particularly in sectors like manufacturing, retail, and distribution. It represents the goods and materials held for resale or production. Effective inventory management is crucial for satisfying customer demand without excessive stock, which can tie up capital and lead to inefficiencies.

Types of Inventories

Inventory is typically categorized into several types based on its role in the production and sales cycle:

- **Raw Materials**: Basic inputs used in manufacturing goods. For instance, wood is a primary raw material in furniture manufacturing.

- **Work-in-Process (WIP)**: Goods that are in the manufacturing process but are not yet complete. Some production activities have transformed the raw materials, but the product is not yet finished or ready for sale.

- **Finished Goods**: Products fully manufactured and ready for sale. In retail, these are the items displayed for customer purchase.

Inventory Management Concerns

Effective inventory management involves navigating challenges such as:

- **Understocking**: Insufficient inventory can result in lost sales and tarnished reputation. A retail store regularly running out of popular items might lose customers to competitors.

- **Overstocking**: Excessive inventory can lead to obsolete stock, higher storage costs, and tied-up capital. For example, a tech company overestimating demand for a new smartphone might face unsold units that depreciate quickly.

Modern inventory practices emphasize sustainability, aiming to minimize waste and environmental impact, especially in fast-moving industries like fashion and electronics. Companies optimize inventory levels, recycle unsold products, and adopt sustainable sourcing to mitigate excess and waste.

Just-In-Time (JIT) Inventory Management

The JIT strategy minimizes inventory by timing the receipt of goods to match production needs. While JIT can reduce costs, it requires precise supplier coordination. The automotive industry, for instance, uses JIT to manage the complex balance of parts needed for vehicle assembly, reducing unnecessary inventory and associated costs.

Inventory Turnover

This metric indicates how quickly a company sells its inventory. A high turnover rate suggests efficient management, while a low rate may indicate overstocking or slow-moving goods. In perishable sectors like food and beverages, optimizing inventory turnover is crucial to minimize waste and enhance profitability.

Inventory Valuation

Accurate inventory valuation is vital for determining the Cost of Goods Sold (COGS) and reporting inventory on financial statements:

- **Specific Identification**: Tracks the cost of each specific item, ideal for unique or high-value items like jewelry or luxury cars.

- **First-In, First-Out (FIFO)**: Assumes the oldest stock is sold first, beneficial in rising price scenarios as it results in lower COGS and higher net income.

- **Last-In, First-Out (LIFO)**: Assumes the newest stock is sold first, useful in inflationary times as it can reduce taxable income due to higher COGS.

- **Average Cost**: Averages the cost of all items to smooth out price fluctuations.

Effective inventory management is crucial for operational efficiency, enhancing customer satisfaction, and ensuring financial stability within any business. This critical aspect of business operations involves a comprehensive understanding of various inventory types, each serving distinct functions across the production and sales cycles. Mastery in managing these types requires businesses to recognize and skillfully address common inventory concerns that can significantly impact their operational health and customer relations.

The strategic leveraging of advanced technology plays a pivotal role in modern inventory management. Implementing state-of-the-art systems for real-time tracking, automated reordering, and accurate demand forecasting can transform traditional inventory practices, reducing risks of overstocking and understocking. These technologies ensure that inventory levels are maintained at optimal levels, thereby maximizing efficiency and responsiveness to market changes.

Additionally, choosing the right inventory valuation method is essential for precise financial reporting and effective cost management. The selection of FIFO (First In, First Out), LIFO (Last In, First Out), or Average Cost methods can significantly impact financial metrics such as the cost of goods sold, tax obligations, and overall profitability. Each method has its unique benefits and is appropriate depending on the specific circumstances of the business and prevailing economic conditions.

Incorporating sustainable practices into inventory management is becoming increasingly important. Businesses are now expected to minimize waste and environmental impact, necessitating practices

217

that extend beyond mere efficiency to include ethical considerations of resource use and disposal. This approach aligns with global sustainability goals and resonates with a growing segment of environmentally conscious consumers.

In summary, robust inventory management is foundational to a company's ability to efficiently operate, meet market demand, and maintain profitability. It directly influences customer satisfaction by ensuring product availability and timely fulfillment of orders. By advancing their inventory practices, businesses can achieve greater financial stability, adapt to market and technological changes, and uphold both economic and environmental responsibilities. Properly managed inventory systems are thus not merely a component of operational strategy but a significant driver of long-term success and sustainability in today's competitive business landscape.

Summary

Effective financial management is essential for the success of any organization. This chapter has demonstrated that finance for non-finance professionals extends far beyond basic number crunching. It involves employing budgeting and forecasting not just as accounting exercises, but as strategic tools vital for informed decision-making, efficient resource allocation, and insightful long-term planning.

Budgeting acts as a comprehensive financial roadmap, enabling organizations to set precise objectives and effectively allocate resources to fulfill these goals. This process is crucial for structuring the management of daily operations, aligning expenditures with strategic priorities, and upholding financial discipline.

Forecasting works together with budgeting, giving organizations the foresight to anticipate future financial scenarios and strategically adapt their plans. Whether facing global crises or planning for market expansions, adept forecasting is crucial for capitalizing on opportunities and minimizing risks. Maintaining current forecasts ensures that organizations can respond with agility to evolving market conditions.

Moreover, this chapter has covered essential topics such as understanding financial statements, the nuances of capital budgeting, and the implications of depreciation and inventory on financial planning. Each topic contributes to a robust understanding of financial management, equipping non-finance professionals with the knowledge to engage deeply with these concepts.

The insights into different budget types, key accounting terminology, advanced forecasting techniques, and the strategic use of tools like ERP systems are invaluable. These elements enable non-finance professionals to make informed decisions that enhance the financial stability and sustainability of their organizations.

By integrating the principles and techniques discussed throughout this chapter, readers are empowered to play a pivotal role in their organization's financial planning and management. The application of this knowledge fosters a proactive approach to financial issues, supports sustainable growth, and drives successful outcomes.

As non-finance professionals master these critical financial practices, they contribute to their immediate teams and the broader organizational context, ensuring that financial strategies are realistic and effective in meeting the complex demands of modern business.

Conclusion

As we conclude our journey through "The Seven Principles for Professional Excellence," it is clear that the skills we have explored are critical for anyone aiming to achieve professional success. Each chapter has established a solid foundation, addressing key areas from mastering time management to enhancing interpersonal communication and embodying your organization's values. These elements form the bedrock of a successful and fulfilling career.

Throughout this book, we have taken a deliberate and strategic approach to personal and professional development. For instance, effective meetings are not just about following an agenda—they are about fostering an environment where ideas thrive, decisions are made efficiently, and everyone is acknowledged and respected. Similarly, mastering negotiation is about more than achieving favorable terms; it is about cultivating enduring relationships grounded in mutual trust and respect. We have explored how these critical skills contribute significantly to sustained professional advancement and success.

In today's fast-paced and unpredictable business world, the skills to adeptly solve problems and make informed decisions are crucial. Critical thinking, precise evaluation of options, and decisive action are more vital than ever. Whether navigating financial limitations highlighted in the chapter "Finance for Non-Finance Professionals" or leading a team through transformative changes, the strategies provided here aim to align your efforts with your organization's broader goals and ethical standards. This book serves as a compass in your pursuit of strategic mastery and leadership excellence, equipping you with the tools needed to thrive under various economic pressures.

The principles outlined in "The Seven Principles for Professional Excellence" are not merely theoretical—they are practical, actionable strategies applicable to daily professional scenarios. Whether you are steering a meeting, brokering a deal, or managing your daily tasks, these principles guide you to approach your responsibilities with clarity, purpose, and professionalism. Each chapter of this book has been crafted to act as a stepping stone towards realizing these goals, offering a clear path forward in the complex maze of professional challenges.

As this book concludes, remember that professional success is not a static achievement but an ongoing journey of learning, growth, and adaptation. The skills and strategies discussed here are crucial, yet they demand continual practice, refinement, and application. Embracing these practices helps you achieve your career goals and inspires others around you to strive for excellence. With every challenge faced and every skill acquired, you progress steadily toward becoming a model of professional excellence and leadership.

I encourage you to confidently use the principles from this book to advance your professional success. Whether you are starting out or experienced, these insights will help you navigate workplace complexities and lead with integrity. Equipped with these tools, you are ready to achieve remarkable results and make a lasting impact on your path to professional excellence. Let this book be your guide as you continue to explore the vast opportunities for personal and professional development, ensuring a legacy of success and influence that extends beyond mere professional achievements.

Index